A RUMOR OF WAR

CHRIST'S MILLENNIAL REIGN AND THE RAPTURE OF HIS CHURCH

And ye shall hear of wars and rumors of war: see that ye be not troubled...
— Matthew 24:6

This book is respectfully dedicated to Bishop Kallistos Ware for speaking words of fire to my heart.

"To the author who has toiled in words . . . be reconciliation in rest."

—St. Ephraim the Syrian,
Hymn for the Feast of the Epiphany

A RUMOR OF WAR

CHRIST'S MILLENNIAL REIGN AND THE RAPTURE OF HIS CHURCH

By

Dennis Eugene Engleman

ISBN 1-928653-07-3

Cover Illustration: "St. John the Evangelist," S. Apollinare in Classe, Ravenna Italy (4th c. mosaic) used by permission.

For a catalogue of our other fine Orthodox publications, contact us at:

Regina Orthodox Press
P.O. Box 5288
Salisbury, MA 01952
1-800-636-2470
FAX: 1-978-462-5079

www.reginaorthodoxpress.com

TABLE OF CONTENTS

INTRODUCTION

At church one Sunday a boy sat in the pew by his mother listening to their preacher deliver a long and fiery sermon. It seemed to this young fellow that the very rafters shook with the force of preacher's exposition, and he stopped squirming with discomfort long enough to glance around at the amazed expressions of others in the church. Then he leaned over and whispered, "Mom, I want to be a preacher when I grow up."

His surprised mother smiled at him with pleasure. "That's wonderful, son. Did the pastor's sermon inspire your decision?"

"Nah," he admitted. "I just figured that since I'm going to be in church anyway, I'd rather stand up and yell than sit down and be quiet."

Unlike the boy in this story, the author of this volume is far more willing to sit down and be quiet than stand up and yell, especially when approaching subjects of spiritual substance. In fact, he would gladly adopt Rufinus' deferential protestations to Bishop Laurentius: "My mind has as little inclination for writing as sufficiency, most faithful Bishop Laurentius, for I well know that it is a matter of no little peril to submit a slender ability to general criticism."

Therefore a few words may be in order regarding why this volume came to be. In the first place, the subject of Christ's millennial reign and the rapture of the Church is one in which many people are extremely interested — perhaps always, but especially in our times. It is also a subject that has given rise to many divergent opinions concerning what is expected to befall various people in particular and mankind in general. Although a variety of interpretations about the last days have been popularized and publicized in the last century, only in our days has the power of worldwide publishing, television, motion picture and internet media enabled the rapid indoctrinating of millions of people with prophetic ideas. Unfortunately, very little of what comes to the public's attention by way of last days themes is Orthodox in character.

In the second place, at a moment in his life when this author believed that, due to his limited grasp of spiritual subjects, he should not dare put pen to paper again, Bishop Kallistos Ware said the following words to him: "May God bless you to continue writing!" Immediately afterwards, the germ of an idea occurred to him which he has subsequently endeavored to articulate, and the result is this book.

Jesus is Coming Again!

The first coming of Jesus Christ to earth—His nativity—was a private affair witnessed by few. On the other hand, His departure from earth, the Ascension, was seen by many. After the Lord's death and resurrection, when He had been with his disciples and teaching them privately for forty days, something unprecedented suddenly occurred, for, "while they beheld, he was taken up; and a cloud received him out of their sight" (Acts 1:9).

This very public return to God the Father was undoubtedly intended to bolster faith in that spiritual heaven to which the Lord calls all people, and to give His followers a visible demonstration of what they should expect at His return. Their amazement at such a sight is understandable, nevertheless some seemingly bemused angels broke the spell:

> While they looked steadfastly toward heaven as he went up, behold, two men stood by them in white apparel; which also said, ye men of Galilee, why stand ye gazing up into heaven? This same Jesus, which is taken up from you into heaven, shall so come in like manner as ye have seen him go into heaven (Acts 1:10-11).

The Lord often referred to His return. Indeed, this topic is one of the most prominent in the New Testament. And although the exact time of that Second Advent remains a mystery, God wishes mankind to be alert and avoid complaisance. Jesus tells us to watch for Him, and emphasizes that He will come quickly, a phrase used six times in the Book of Revelation: "Behold, I come quickly" (Rev. 22:7).

After a delay of two thousand years however, we may reasonably conclude that "quickly" does not signify a short duration as man counts time, but rather the suddenness and unexpectedness of the event for those who are not prepared. "Repent; or else I will come unto thee quickly," says the Lord (Rev. 2:16). Logically, one would expect Christ to "come quickly" to succor Christians who through repentance have demonstrated their love for Him. But no, it is to the faithless that have *not* repented, and have *not* done the first works of virtue, that He shall come quickly: "Repent, and do the first works; or else I will come unto thee quickly" (Rev. 2:5).

Through this we can clearly comprehend that a fundamental characteristic of Christ's Second Advent will be its unexpectedness. He shall come as a thief, that is, unbeknownst to those who are intruded upon. "If, therefore, thou shalt not watch, I will come upon thee as a thief, and thou shalt not know what hour I will come upon thee," the Lord warns (Rev. 3:3).

It is therefore not necessary to conceive that Jesus may return at any possible moment (which is a tenet of premillennialist doctrine), for whenever He *does* come, it will be a shock and a surprise to those who do not live in a state of continual repentance. In other words, His return is perpetually immanent, regardless of how many prophetic signs are given and fulfilled in anticipation of it. "Whether the End comes late or soon in our human time-scale, it is always *immanent*, always spiritually close at hand," says Bishop Kallistos Ware. "We are to have in our hearts a sense of urgency."[1]

Things Too Wonderful

"I uttered that I understood not; things too wonderful for me, which I knew not," lamented Job after his conversation with God (Job 42:3). One may easily share

---

[1] Bishop Kallistos Ware, *The Orthodox Way*, Crestwood, NY: St. Vladimir's Seminary Press, 1999, p. 134.

Job's sense of impoverished comprehension, especially when attempting to speak of those things concerning the kingdom of God. Yet Christians have an aid to their understanding that this Old Testament figure lacked, and that is the Holy Church.

What is the Holy Church? Protestant writers (who typically affirm modern premillennialist doctrines) conceive the "Church" as being nothing more than Roman Catholicism, against which they have not stopped protesting after 500 years. Yet they conceive the "church" as "those who became temples of the Holy Spirit when converted,"[2] or as "everyone who has ever accepted Jesus Christ as Lord and Savior."[3] In so doing, they define the organization in which they affirm membership in terms of men rather than of God.

Unfortunately, neither of these conceptions permits reliance on that wondrous body of Christian tradition that affirms that "He [Christ] is the head of the body, the church" (Col. 1:18), and through which the Holy Spirit has actually been ceaselessly operative since apostolic times, and namely Orthodox Christianity.

In addition, the vague definitions of Protestantism have allowed many who imagined themselves possessed of the Spirit to spew out opinionated concepts that, in turn, have produced further divisions among those supposedly united in their understanding of Scriptures. Martin Luther initiated the Protestant Ref-

[2] Tim LaHaye, *Rapture [Under Attack]* (Sisters, OR: Multnomah Publishers, 1992), p. 231.
[3] Peter & Patti LaLonde, *Left Behind* (Eugene, OR: Harvest House Publishers, 1995), p. 94.

ormation by putting forward the notion that every believer is capable of interpreting Scripture correctly all by himself. Yet even in Luther's lifetime several protesting groups disagreed and departed from *him*, and today there are more than 20,000 Protestant denominations. One cannot but conclude that this history of discord indicates a flawed premise.

The Lord Himself said little that is recorded in the Gospels about the nature and makeup of His Church, and yet the attempt to define who was, and who was not, to be considered part of this privileged body has been behind nearly all Christian infighting. The author has no desire to prolong that regrettable situation through anything written in this book. It is not necessary that "I" know whether "you" are in the Church (or vice-versa). It is only necessary that Christ knows — and this He assuredly does, for He says, "I know whom I have chosen" (John 13:18). From this we may understand that the Lord "knows," or is in intimate relationship with, those whom He has chosen to participate in His blessed life.

To Know and Be Known of God

To know someone is to have a personal relationship with that person. We may know *of* a particular individual, but we do not *know* him or her until we have become personally acquainted. At that point some kind of bond occurs, whether friendly or hostile, and even if we never cast eyes upon the person again for fifty years, we can say without hesitation, "I know so-and-so."

Likewise, we may know of Jesus, but this is not the same as knowing Jesus. Of course, one cannot claim familiar acquaintance with the Son of God like one can with just anybody, nevertheless it is clear from the Scriptures and the lives of saints that intimate communion with God is at the heart of all true spiritual experience.

But how is this intimate communion and personal relationship to be achieved? Our Lord answers with a prayer to His own Father in heaven:

> Neither pray I for these alone, but for them also who shall believe on me through their word; that they all may be one, as thou, Father, art in me, and I in thee, that they also may be one in us; that the world may believe that thou hast sent me (John 17:21).

The Lord desires that we be united with one another in faith with Him, for this unity will convict the world of the truth of the Gospel. Herein is cause for shame among divided Christians, for their disunity has born the opposite witness.

Unity with the Church

Orthodox Christians believe that the unity for which Christ prayed starts with humble submission among His followers to the Church He founded — which exists unto this day. Being the Bride of Christ and the Body of Christ, the Church is a living entity whose mysterious nature may not be reduced to simple phrases, however seemingly true. It is composed, to be sure, of those who accepted Jesus Christ as savior and became temples of the Holy Spirit when converted. Yet it is very much more than this. For one thing, it is also composed of those multitudes of saints, martyrs, and others who have lived Godly lives and abide now in heaven.

How are Christians to know whether they are actually in the Church? Belief is fundamental, of course, but this is merely the first step. The farmer does not plant unless he believes he will later reap the harvest. But such faith alone is not sufficient to gain that harvest. He must still plant, and cultivate, and otherwise toil according to the ancient craft of horticulture in order to produce tangible fruits. Similarly, one does not become a representative of Congress, or quarterback of the Atlanta Falcons, or president of Ford Motor Company, merely by believing it to be so. Much more in spiritual matters than in material or intellectual ones, specific behaviors must attend our belief if we wish to realize genuine results.

The Church, being the foretaste of heaven on earth, is not entered haphazardly or by a side door, but through the Gate. "I am the door; by me if any man enter in, he shall be saved, and shall go in and out, and find pasture" (John 10:9). Here, in the pasture of the Church are sacramental initiations, liturgical worship and holy tradition. Such practices deriving from apostolic times have inherent meaning that cannot be dismissed without consequence, regardless of whether these are explicitly mentioned in the canonical Scriptures. Making the sign of the Cross, for instance, reciting the creed and reverencing icons, have profound spiritual meaning for the human soul.

Understanding within the Church

Thus we must search for understanding in the light of the Church. While this is true in all arenas, it is particularly important in the realm of prophecy. For here, where prophetic language is often rife with metaphor and the cloak of obscurity and mystification hide future events from clear view, speculation and sensationalism can run rampant. It is a serious mishap if by vain imaginings we deceive ourselves; but if we deceive others, however unintentionally, the consequences are severe. "Whoso shall offend one of these little ones which believe in me," says Jesus, "it were better for him that a millstone were hanged about his neck, and that he were drowned in the depth of the sea" (Mat. 18: 5).

Therefore, in reading the Bible, we should of course believe that God speaks to us personally through the venerable text, and that He is imparting a unique message for a particular person at that distinct time and place. Yet we must not base opinions on this premise alone. However inspired we may be, however confidant even that heaven is revealing divine mysteries, we are not entitled to trust our own impressions in the matter. For we must *also* read as a member of the Church, as one of but many Christians who have read before. Our particular view of the Scriptures must be informed and guided by the light of those others. In the final analysis, if our understanding is at odds with, and contradictory to, what has been received and believed by the Church since apostolic times, then we have read amiss.

To Be Patient with Ignorance

And finally, we must also accept that our understanding will never be total and complete, at least in this life. Were one as wise as Solomon, he would still not comprehend all God's mysteries. "Let us not then be impatient to learn all things, but let us endure to be even ignorant of some things, that when we have found a teacher, we may not afford him a double toil," counsels St. John Chrysostom. "Many oftentimes have remained incurably diseased, by carelessly entangling themselves in evil opinions."[4]

We must be patient with our ignorance and not over-confidant of mere human knowledge. "If any man think that he knoweth anything, he knoweth nothing yet as he ought to know," says St. Paul (1 Cor. 8:2). We should seek not the *knowledge* of intellectualization, but rather the *knowing* of relationship—that is, love. "If any man love God, the same is known of him," the apostle continues (1 Cor. 8:3).

The way of Christianity is at essence direct and simple—a fool could do it (and of course, Christianity is considered foolish by the world). Yet at the same time it requires all and everything—the "death" of man as an

---

[4] John Chrysostom, *Homilies on the Gospel According to Saint Matthew*, LXXV, 4.

isolated individual. For it is the way of actually loving God. "Ultimately, the only law that Christ gave to man was the law of love," says Hieromonk Damascene.

> Having this law "in their inward parts," his followers would obey God's law naturally, spontaneously, without always having to think, to choose, and to worry over legalistic formulas. "You shall love the Lord your God," He said, "with all your heart, and with all your soul, and with all your mind; and you shall love your neighbor as yourself. On these two commandments hang all the law and the prophets."[5]

Searching Diligently and Urgently

As there are more Biblical references to the last days than to nearly any other theme, it behooves us to consider this subject seriously and consistently. As Metropolitan Ephraim of Boston writes, "More than any other time before us, it is necessary for us to do the work of the Lord more diligently and with greater urgency."[6]

Regarding prophetic events, and especially those relating to that culminating point of sacred history called the Day of the Lord, it would be pretentious in-

[5] Damascene (Christensen), *Christ the Eternal Tao* (Platina CA: Valaam Books, 1999), p. 268.

[6] "On the New Millennium, An Encyclical to the Faithful," *Orthodox Christian Witness*, 35:8 (August 2001), p. 6.

deed for any mortal to claim a comprehensive understanding. The author hopes to simply set forth in the following pages what Orthodox thinking on these crucial subjects has been and is, and thus enable readers to vitalize their own awareness with the patristic mind. It shall be necessary in the course of this examination to contrast Orthodox with non-Orthodox teaching. And although it is the author's personal conviction that Orthodoxy bears the Holy Spirit more fully, and Christian doctrine more truly, than other confessions, he by no means wishes to disparage any person or faith that honors the name of Jesus Christ.

CHAPTER ONE

The Creation of Sentient Beings

The essence of "being" is "be." Ultimately, a being is one who is. And yet the Scriptures entitle us to say more, namely, a being is one who is and who *knows* that he is. God describes Himself thus, for He says, "I am that I am." God is fully conscious that He is.

According to this definition irrational animals and plants are not beings, for although they are, they do not know that they are. They have consciousness, but it is not self-consciousness. They may even have personalities, but they are not persons. Personhood, which includes conscience, will, and self-determination, belongs to the realm of being.

It appears from the Scriptures that there are only two kinds of created beings: angels and men. Heaven is named first in the order of creation, and presumably included in this are the creatures inhabiting heaven. Although there is no specific mention of God's creating the angelic host, this may be implied in the words "all the host of them" (Gen. 2:1).

Through this the fathers understand that angels were created before mankind: "The Angels, Dominions, and Powers, although they began to exist at some time, were already in existence when the world was created," wrote St. Ambrose:

> For all things "were created, things visible and things invisible, whether Thrones or Dominions or Principalities or Powers. All things," we are told, "have been created through and unto Him" (Col. 1:16)[7]

The Nature of Angels

God formed immaterial creatures to rejoice in His infinite love. These invisible beings are composed, so far as humans can comprehend, of intelligence alone: "It appears, indeed, that even before this world an order of things existed of which our mind can form an idea, but of which we can say nothing, because it is too lofty a subject for men who are but beginners and are still babes in knowledge," says St. Basil.[8]

John of Damascus describes angels as incorporeal. They were not formed from the dust of the earth, as was Adam, therefore our knowledge of them remains limited. Nevertheless, in comparison with God, even these are dense and material:

> An angel, then, is an intelligent essence, in perpetual motion, with free-will, incorporeal, ministering to God, having obtained by grace

[7] Ambrose, *Six Days*, I, 5, p. 18.
[8] Basil the Great, *Hexaemeron*, I, 5.

an immortal nature: and the Creator alone
knows the form and limitation of its essence.[9]

Free Will

As angels are frequently portrayed doing God's
bidding without reluctance or reservation, it is easy to
form the opinion that they are merely spiritual
automatons or etheric robots with no minds of their
own. This is incorrect, however. Angels and men share
some common characteristics, one of the most fundamental of these being free will. Self-volition is an
attribute bestowed by God from the beginning, according Justin Martyr: "God in the beginning made the
race of angels and men with free will."[10]

Being sentient and self-conscious, men and angels
have the capacity—and the obligation—to choose between right and wrong. The meaning of free will is
different for men and for angels, however:

> As it is rational and intelligent, it is endowed
> with free-will: and as it is created, it is change-
> able, having power either to abide or progress
> in goodness, or to turn towards evil. It is not
> susceptible of repentance because it is incorpo-

---

[9] John of Damascus, *An Exact Exposition of the Orthodox Faith*,
II, 3.

[10] Justin Martyr, "The Second Apology," *The Ante-Nicene Fathers*, vol. 1, (Grand Rapids: Eerdmans Publishing Co., 1975), p.
190.

real. For it is owing to the weakness of his body that man comes to have repentance.[11]

The Fall of Lucifer

The heavens and the earth were made good from the beginning. Moses goes into some detail about God's creative process so we may appreciate how carefully and lovingly these realms and inhabitants were established. "And God saw the thing that he had made, and behold, it was very good" (Gen. 1:31).

The goodness of being carries with it an awesome responsibility—that of right choice. Free will is at the bottom of one of the most perplexing and riveting stories of the Bible. It is difficult to imagine that one blessed to be near God could ever turn away from Him, but this is what the Scriptures teach. It is said that the highest and most beautiful of God's angels was a cherubim called Lucifer.

Apparently dazzled by his own glory, Lucifer became proud. "If you will understand what kind of sin the devil committed, and what kind Adam [later] committed, you will find nothing else but pride alone," wrote St. Symeon the New Theologian. "But the devil and Adam became proud by reason of the great glory which they were vouchsafed in abundance."[12]

---

[11] John of Damascus, *An Exact Exposition of the Orthodox Faith*, II, 3.

[12] Symeon the New Theologian, *The First Created Man*, Platina, CA: St. Herman of Alaska Brotherhood, 1994, p. 68

So like unto the Lord Himself was Lucifer that he conceived the desire of being even greater than God. But self-exaltation leads directly to abasement, as the Lord warned. "How art thou fallen from heaven, O Lucifer, son of the morning! For thou hast said in thine heart, I will exalt my throne above the stars of God, I will be like the Most High" (Isaiah 14:12-14).

Heaven consists in preferring God's will, and hell consists in preferring one's own will. This also is the simple meaning of humility and pride. Lucifer preferred his own will to the will of God. In so doing he voluntary abdicated heaven and entered the state of hell. As St. John Cassian says,

> For as Lucifer was endowed with divine splendour, and shone forth among the other higher powers by the bounty of his Maker, he believed that he had acquired the splendour of that wisdom and the beauty of those powers, with which he was graced by the gift of the Creator, by the might of his own nature, and not by the beneficence of His generosity. And on this account he was puffed up as if he stood in no need of divine assistance in order to continue in this state of purity, and esteemed himself to be like God, as if, like God, he had no need of any one, and trusting in the power of his own will, fancied that through it he could richly supply himself with everything which was necessary for the consummation of virtue or for the per-

petuation of perfect bliss. This thought alone was the cause of his first fall.[13]

It is difficult to fathom self-deception of this magnitude—for Lucifer must of necessity have deceived himself first. Unlike us, he had no tempter to blame for his fall, no human weakness or passionate inclination. He could not be ignorant of the nature of reality and the imagined possibility of hiding his sin. He who had been next to God chose to oppose his creator. He who had been in the embrace of limitless Love chose instead the emptiness of self-love. "Those who were foreknown to be unrighteous, whether men or angels, are not made wicked by God's fault, but each man by his own fault is what he will appear to be," says Justin Martyr.[14]

Being pure intelligence, and with no evil mentor to tempt into sinful behavior, the effect of this willful rejection of God was stark and dramatic. Lucifer could not merely be a little proud or somewhat evil. "He that is not with me is against me," said the Lord about Satan (Mat. 12:30). Lucifer must either be totally with God, or totally against Him, and he chose the latter. St. Gregory of Nyssa described this in terms of a rock hurtling down from a mountain ridge under the power of gravitational attraction:

> When once he, who by his apostasy from goodness had begotten in himself this envy, had received this bias to evil, like a rock, torn

[13] John Cassian, *Institutes*, IV.

[14] Justin Martyr, "Dialogue with Trypho," *The Ante-Nicene Fathers*, vol. 1, p.269.

asunder from a mountain ridge, which is driven down headlong by its own weight, in like manner he, dragged away from his original natural propensity to goodness and gravitating with all his weight in the direction of vice, was deliberately forced and borne away as by a kind of gravitation to the utmost limit of iniquity...[15]

A War in Heaven

A sign of Lucifer's heavenly preeminence is the general angelic confusion and debilitation that followed in the wake of his fall. In the book of Revelation he is described as a red dragon whose tail draws down a substantial portion of the heavenly host.

And there appeared another wonder in heaven; behold, a great red dragon, having seven heads and ten horns, and seven crowns upon his heads. And his tail drew the third part of the stars of heaven, and did cast them to the earth (Revelation 12:3,4).

The "stars of heaven" represent lower orders of angels, deceived by the great deceiver into joining his rebellion against God. According to St. John, a third of the heavenly host were cast down to earth in that great contest. In human terms this must be an extraordinarily large number, for the prophet Daniel saw in a vision

[15] Gregory of Nyssa, *The Great Catechism*, VI.

that "thousand thousands ministered unto Him [God], and ten thousand times ten thousand stood before Him" (Daniel 7:10). St. Cyril of Jerusalem explains that the numbers would certainly be vastly larger, except, "... the Prophet could not express more than these."[16]

The result of this colossal rift is described as a war in heaven, in which Lucifer and the angels who followed him were defeated and removed. Although this scene is presented in the last book of the Bible, we understand that it happened before the dawn of mankind:

> And there was war in heaven: Michael and his angels fought against the dragon; and the dragon fought and his angels, and prevailed not; neither was their place found anymore in heaven. And the great dragon was cast out, that old serpent, called the Devil, and Satan, which deceiveth the whole world: he was cast out into the earth, and his angels were cast out with him (Rev. 12:7-9).

This heavenly discord set the stage not only for man's creation, but also for his own subsequent rebellion in response the Satan's temptation. Bishop Kallistos Ware writes,

> The devil [is] the first among those angels who turned from God to the hell of self-will. There has been a double fall: first the angels, and then of man. For Orthodoxy the fall of angels is not a picturesque fairy-tale but spiritual truth. Prior

---

[16] Cyril of Jerusalem, *Catechetical Lectures*, XV: 24.

to man's creation, there had already occurred a parting of the ways within the noetic realm: some of the angels remained steadfast in obedience to God, others rejected him.[17]

In addition, the "seven heads and ten horns" links this dragon to the Antichrist (see my book, *Ultimate Things: An Orthodox Christian Perspective on the End Times*): "I saw a woman sit upon a scarlet colored beast, full of names of blasphemy, having seven heads and ten horns" (Rev. 17:3). Here, the rebellion against God, which began in heaven, will culminate in earth.

The Power of Demons

Though darkened, the fallen angels are nevertheless extraordinarily powerful. These demons are able to affect others by means of their acute spiritual intelligence. Origen writes:

> The term "demons" is always applied to those wicked powers, freed from the encumbrance of a grosser body, who lead men astray, and fill them with distractions, and drag them down from God and supercelestial thoughts to things here below.[18]

Modern man, deluded by his own vain impression of self-sophistication, typically regards tales of demons

---

[17] Bishop Kallistos Ware, *The Orthodox Way*, p. 57.
[18] Origen, "Against Celcus," 5, *The Ante-Nicene Fathers*, vol. 4, p. 545.

as fantasy. Nevertheless, countless trustworthy witnesses have affirmed their reality. St. Seraphim of Sarov, a miracle worker of the nineteenth century, is celebrated for battling evil powers for one thousand days and nights while he prayed kneeling upon a flat rock. When one of his spiritual sons jokingly wondered if devils have claws, he replied,

> Don't you know that the devils have no claws? They have been represented with hoofs, horns and tails because it is impossible for the human imagination to conceive anything more hideous. And they really are hideous, for their conscious desertion of God and their voluntary resistance to divine grace made them, who before the fall, were Angels of light, angels of such darkness and abomination that they cannot be portrayed in any human likeness. Still some likeness is necessary; that is why they are represented as black and ugly.[19]

Permanent Non-Repentance

Can anything make devils feel sorry for their choices? If not, it is clear why man is considered a greater and more complex creation than the angels, and why Satan is envious and bitter. For man has the capacity for suffering. He can experience loss and disappointment, grief and pain. He can perceive the

[19] Archimandrite Lazarus Moore, *St. Seraphim of Sarov: A Spiritual Biography* (Blanco, TX: New Sarov Press, 1994), p. 210.

part his own self-will has played in producing his un-happiness, and he can repent of the evil in his heart. St. John of Damascus writes,

> For through his incorruption the devil, when he had fallen as the result of his own free choice, was firmly established in wickedness, so that there was no room for repentance and no hope of change: just as, moreover, the angels also, when they had made free choice of virtue be-came through grace immovably rooted in goodness.[20]

St. Ignatius Brianchaninov explains that it was the devil's temptation of mankind that finally set the cos-mic die, so to speak. The fallen angels had turned from God, but it was only after they had injured man that God turned from them:

> The crime committed by the fallen angels against men finally decided the fate of the fallen angels. The mercy and grace of God was finally withdrawn from them, and they set the seal on their fall. [21]

Giants in the Earth

The Bible speaks of a race of giants, also called the "sons of God." These powerful but immoral beings

[20] *An Exact Exposition of the Orthodox Faith*, II, 30.

[21] Bishop Ignatius Brianchaninov, *The Arena* (Jordanville, NY: Holy Trinity Monastery, 1983), p. 186.

spread evil throughout the earth, for which cause God sent the great Flood:

> There were giants in the earth in those days; and also after that, when the sons of God came in unto the daughters of men, and they bare children to them, the same became mighty men which were of old, men of renown. And God saw that the wickedness of man was great in the earth, and that every imagination of the thoughts of his heart was only evil continually (Gen. 6:4-5).

Justin Martyr says that it was these demons fallen from heaven which came into the daughters of men and thus magnified their contamination of evil so greatly among mankind.

> God, when He had made the whole world... committed the care of men and of all things under heaven to angels whom He appointed over them. But the angels transgressed this appointment, and were captivated by love of women, and begat children who are those that are called demons; and besides, they afterwards subdued the human race to themselves... and among men they sowed murders, wars, adulteries, intemperate deeds, and all wickedness.[22]

Perhaps the beauty of Eve played a role in her temptation by the serpent in the Garden of Eden. In any

---

[22] Justin Martyr, "The Second Apology," p. 190.

case, there seems to have been an interaction between men and angels that was irregular. Commodianus writes,

> When almighty God, to beautify the nature of the world, willed that the earth should be visited by angels, when they were sent down they despised His laws. Such was the beauty of women, that it turned them aside; so that, being contaminated, they could not return to heaven. Rebels from God, they uttered words against Him. Then the Highest uttered His judgment against them; and from their seed giants are said to have been born. By them arts were made known in the earth...and when they died, men erected images... and it is such as these especially that ye this day worship and pray to as gods.[23]

---

[23] Commodianus, "The Instructions of Commodianus in Favour of Christian Discipline," *The Ante-Nicene Fathers,* vol. 4, p. 203.

CHAPTER TWO

Man:
The Younger Brother

A young man was out for a stroll on a summer evening. In the distance he saw a lamppost, its lamp sending friendly streams of light onto the sidewalk below. Groveling at the foot of the lamppost was old man, crying out as one suffering grave misfortune. The young man hurried to offer assistance.

"What is wrong, sir?" the young gentleman asked. "Are you injured?"

"No, praise God! I am in excellent health."

"Then why do you cry out so lamentably?" the newcomer asked.

At this the old man sighed heavily and cast anxious glances in every direction. "Because I have lost what is to me the most precious object in the world!"

"That is terrible," the young man responded. "I shall help you look for it!" He dropped to his knees and began to crawl about the circle of flickering light that illumined the sidewalk.

Together they searched for over an hour, at first randomly, then methodically by sectors one foot square. At last the exhausted helper stood, stretched his stiff back and said, "If only we knew exactly where you were when the object was lost."

"Of course I know where I was," the old man replied with indignation.

At this the other brightened. "And where was that?"

The old man waved his hand indefinitely into the darkness beyond their view. "Over there," he said, without interrupting his search.

"What?" the young man exclaimed. "Then why are we looking here?"

The old man raised his head, an expression of incredulity on his face.

"Because the light is better here!"

The story can serve to illustrate the human condition, for each person is in need of finding the most precious object in the world. And no matter where we think this has been lost, the only place where it may be found is in the light. From the spiritual point of view, the old man's behavior is not irrational at all. If we conceive of this precious object being our own true selves, then the story is doubly appropriate, for the Scriptures teach that our lives are hidden from us. "Your life is hid with Christ in God," says St. Paul (Co. 3:1).

To illuminate who we are as people, we must base our understanding on God's creation of man. The book of Genesis depicts both the majesty and the humility of man's making. God the Father, speaking to the other persons of the Holy Trinity, said, "Let us make man in our image, after our likeness: and let them have dominion over the fish of the sea, and over the fowl of the air, and over the cattle, and over all the earth, and over every creeping thing that creepeth upon the earth" (Gen. 1:26).

God elected to create a living being in His own divine image, and to endow this unique and wondrous creature with supremacy over all the animals that He had already made. And yet, when God set about bringing man into being, He did not use some kind of high spiritual stuff for his raw materials, but rather the lowest thing available: "And the Lord God formed man of the dust of the ground, and breathed into his nostrils the breath of life; and man became a living soul" (Gen. 2:7).

God combined what was highest with what was lowest to form something new and unprecedented, as St. Gregory the Theologian explains:

> Now the Creator-Word, determining to... produce a single living being out of both (the invisible and the visible creation, I mean) fashions Man. And taking a body from already existing matter, and placing in it a Breath taken from Himself, as a sort of second world, great in littleness, He placed him on the earth, a new Angel.[24]

We can scarcely conceive now of newly created man's original nature. He was no caveman, grunting and clubbing animals with a stick, as modern scientists imagine, but rather vibrant with intelligence and nascent virtue. God intended man to grow in all manner of

---

[24] Gregory the Theologian, *Second Oration on* Easter, 6-7.

excellence, and eventually to take his place among the angels. According to St. Symeon the New Theologian, "God, in the beginning when He created man, created him holy, passionless, and sinless, in His own image and likeness. And... in time they [men] would have ascended into the most perfect glory, and being changed, would have drawn near to God; and the soul of each one would have become light-bearing by reason of the illuminations which would have poured out upon it from the Divinity."[25]

God willed that man should grow in perfection, that he should rise from beneath the angels to be their equal. Saint Augustine of Hippo wrote,

> Man, whose nature was to be a mean between the angelic and the bestial, He created in such sort, that if he remained in subjection to his Creator as his rightful Lord, and piously kept His commandments, he should pass into the company of the angels, and obtain, without the intervention of death, a blessed and endless immortality.[26]

The Garden of Eden

The first created earth was originally very different from what we see today. Like unto the heavens, which

[25] Symeon the New Theologian, *The First Created Man* (Platina, CA: St. Herman of Alaska Brotherhood, 1994), p. 51, 88.

[26] Augustine, *City of God* (New York: The Modern Library, 1950), p. 406.

were created to be a delight for their inhabitants, earth was a place of great beauty, filled with fruit-bearing plants and gentle animals. It was a place of love and life, not fear and death. "For the vultures were not yet looking over the earth at the very moment when the animals were born," says St. Basil.

> Nature had not yet been divided, for it was in all its freshness; hunters did not capture, for such was not yet the practice of men; the beasts, for their part, did not yet tear their prey, for they were not carnivores... But all followed the way of the swans, and all grazed on the grass of the meadow.[27]

Yet, for all earth's wondrousness, primal man was given a better place still, for he was made to live in that most wondrous spot of all, the Garden of Eden:

> And the Lord God planted a garden eastward in Eden; and there he put the man whom he had formed. And out of the ground made the Lord God to grow every tree that is pleasant to the sight, and good for food; the tree of life also in the midst of the garden, and the tree of knowledge of good and evil (Gen. 2:8-9).

Here man reigned as a loving king over all the visible creation. Adam's authority is shown in that God allowed him to name the creatures He had made (Gen. 2:19).

---

[27] Basil the Great, *On the Origin of Man*, 2:6-7.

The Crown of Creation

The authority of primal man is virtually incomprehensible to corrupted modern sensibilities, which view all forms of dominance in terms of advantage and disadvantage, of exploitation and victimization. But God, who reigns over all, set his beloved Adam to be a benevolent ruler — like Himself — over the visible realm: "Before the transgression all things were under his power," wrote St. John of Damascus. "For God set him as ruler over all things on the earth and in the waters."[28]

This power and rule was a natural consequence of an undistracted awareness of God's presence. Adam understood both who he was, and the nature of his relationship to God. There was no discord or conflict in his consciousness, and hence no limitation in the exercise of his abilities. "Physically, they were free from sorrows, illnesses, and death," says Andreyev. "As to the religious-ethical state of the first people, it was a highly blissful and blessed state. Their main happiness consisted of a direct personal communion with God."[29]

Not only was man given to rule all that can be seen and heard and smelled and touched, of which he is the most exalted manifestation, but the visible creation was brought into being solely for his sake. St. Symeon writes, "In this whole visible creation there is nothing higher than man (for everything visible was created for

[28] John of Damascus, *An Exact Exposition of the Orthodox Faith*, II, 10.

[29] I. M. Andreyev, *Orthodox Apologetic Theology* (Platina, CA: St. Herman of Alaska Brotherhood, 1995), p. 132.

man)."[30] Why did God make man, and endow him with such heavenly possibilities and so honor him before the very angels gaze? Indeed, King David asked the same question:

> What is man that thou art mindful of him? For thou hast made him a little lower than the angels, and hast crowned him with glory and honor. Thou hast made him to have dominion over the works of thy hands: thou hast put all things under his feet (Psalm 8:5).

Replacing Fallen Angels in Heaven

It may be that man owes his existence to Lucifer's downfall. The angelic rebellion decimated heaven's ranks by one-third, and these celestial beings needed to be replenished. According to St. Anthony the Great, man was made to fill that vacancy: "God created a new rational creature—man—specifically to replace the fallen angels. God placed man in Paradise, which was in a lower heaven and which was previously under the jurisdiction of the fallen cherub."[31]

That man, a creature "lower than the angels," was destined to assume their place in heaven—this was disgrace and insult to Lucifer and his minions.

The Lord deigned to create man out of dust and with such earthly beings to complete the lack in

---

[30] Symeon the New Theologian, *The First Created Man*, p.47.
[31] Antony the Great, *Conversation on Spirits, Menology*, Jan. 17.

the angelic worlds, which was a consequence of the falling away of the proud spirits. And this was infinite shame and infinite punishment to the proud ones.[32]

God keeps certain things to Himself, such as the time of Christ's Return at the end of the age: "But of that day and hour knoweth no man, no, not the angels of heaven, but my Father only" (Mat. 24:36). And perhaps the creation of man was another such surprise to the angels, for it appears to have taken Lucifer unawares. Satan may have thought to leave God shorthanded by his rebellion, only to learn later that his place in heaven should be given to an upstart. No wonder he was jealous of mankind!

When Lucifer saw that man was capable of occupying the 'empty thrones' abandoned by the fallen angels, he could not endure his disgrace, was inflamed with vicious hatred and envy towards man, and decided to destroy him, beginning to pour out the poison of evil and saying to him, 'You will be as Gods.'"[33]

Ousting Fallen Angels on Earth

Nor was this humiliation all. Not only were the fallen angels' heavenly thrones forfeit, but also even the

---

[32] Quoted by Bishop Nektary, "The Mystical Meaning of the Tsar's Martyrdom," *The Orthodox Word*, 24:5-6 (Sept-Dec 1988), p. 315.

[33] Bishop Nektary, pp. 314-315.

earthly realm to which they had been consigned was given over to man. God placed man in Lucifer's domain, the paradise of earth, and gave him *dominion* over earth and all her creatures (Gen. 1:28-30).

Satan lost heaven, and also lost earth, to a creature that must have seemed inferior to him in every way. Is it any surprise that one so infected with pride would be eternally hostile to man? St. Ignatius explains:

> The reprobate spirits, led by their chief, tried to seduce the newly created men and make them share their fall, and so as to have adherents or associates of the same mind; and they endeavored to infect them with the poison of their hatred for God. In this they succeeded.[34]

Satan Tempts Man

Therefore the stage was set for a great contest, in which God allowed Satan to tempt Adam and Eve. John of Damascus writes,

> It was necessary, therefore, that man should first be put to the test (for man untried and unproved would be worth nothing), and being made perfect by the trial through the observance of the command should thus receive incorruption as the prize of his virtue.[35]

---

[34] Bishop Ignatius Brianchaninov, *The Arena*, p. 185.
[35] John of Damascus, *An Exact Exposition of the Orthodox Faith*, II, 30.

We all know what happened next. Genesis records how the serpent tempted Eve with the promise that by eating of the Tree of the Knowledge of Good and Evil man would become as God. Adam, of course, followed her in this sin (Gen. 3:1-6).

St. Augustine points out that the serpent was not in itself evil, but that Satan used it as his mouthpiece to influence Eve:

> After that proud and therefore envious angel... chose the serpent as his mouthpiece in that bodily Paradise in which it and all the other earthly animals were living with those two human beings. And this animal being subdued to his wicked ends by the presence and superior force of his angelic nature, he abused as his instrument, making his assault upon the weaker part of that human alliance.[36]

Why Did God Permit Evil?

The question is always asked, why did God not simply destroy Satan instead of sending him to earth? Since from this angelic rebellion have proceeded all the miseries of the universe, why did God not instantly eliminate the defectors? Although the problem of evil does not admit of a facile response, we can at least say that God has limitless love for all His created beings.

---

[36] Augustine, *City of God*, p. 458.

Free will could not be free if it did not imply the possibility of disobedience.

Also God, Who is lowest as well as highest, often chooses to discipline by means of humiliation. Therefore He has not destroyed the devil, but given him a weaker adversary whose own vulnerability is his greatest asset, as St. Cyril of Jerusalem explains:

He suffered him [Satan] to live, for two purposes, that he might disgrace himself the more in his defeat, and that mankind might be crowned with victory. O all wise providence of God! which takes the wicked purpose for a groundwork of salvation for the faithful. For as He took the unbrotherly purpose of Joseph's brethren for a groundwork of His own dispensation, and, by permitting them to sell their brother from hatred, took occasion to make him king whom He would; so he permitted the devil to wrestle, that the victors might be crowned; and that when victory was gained, he might be the more disgraced as being conquered by the weaker, and men be greatly honored as having conquered him who was once an Archangel.[37]

But, since God in His mercy allowed the devil to continue existing, why did He at least not sequester the evil spirit in some way? Why was man placed, as it were, directly in Satan's path? From our limited and

---

[37] Cyril of Jerusalem, *Catechetical Lectures*, VIII, 4.

human point of view the contest seems vastly unfair and lopsided in Lucifer's favor. But that is in part because we do not understand and appreciate our own true potential, nor the extraordinary love and confidence our heavenly Father has bestowed upon us. As the Holy Scriptures teach again and again, God delights in choosing the weaker vessel to shame a stronger one. He wills that humility and lowliness shall triumph over pride and self-exaltation. This principle is illustrated throughout the Old Testament. "Since, then, God was not ignorant that man should fall, why should He not have suffered him to be tempted by an angel who hated and envied him?" asks Augustine.

> It was not, indeed, that He was unaware that he should be conquered, but because he foresaw that by the man's seed, aided by divine grace, this same devil himself should be conquered, to the greater glory of the saints.[38]

The Fall of Man

Powerful as he was, Satan could not by brute force compel Adam and Eve. They walked and talked with God, and enjoyed His Company. The devil could not hope to enlist them directly into his abominable cause, therefore he set about to separate them from God by means of their own disobedience. According to St. Gregory of Nyssa,

---

[38] Augustine, *City of God*, New York, p. 476

His plan, therefore, is to withdraw man from this enabling strength, that thus he may be easily captured by him and open to his treachery. As in a lamp when the flame has caught the wick and a person is unable to blow it out, he mixes water with the oil and by this devices will dull the flame, in the same way the enemy, by craftily mixing up badness in man's will, has produced a kind of extinguishment and dullness in the blessing.[39]

Although the symbol of disobedience was eating forbidden fruit, the fathers are explicit in showing that Adam and Eve were actually tempted by that which excited the devil's own lust—namely, the desire to be gods unto themselves: "The envy of the devil then was the reason of man's fall," says John of Damascus.

For that same demon, so full of envy and with such a hatred of good, would not suffer us to enjoy the pleasures of heaven, when he himself was kept below on account of his arrogance, and hence the false one tempts miserable man with the hope of Godhead, and leading him up to as great a height of arrogance as himself, he hurls him down into a pit of destruction just as deep.[40]

[39] Gregory of Nyssa, *The Great Catechism*, VI.
[40] John of Damascus, *An Exact Exposition of the Orthodox Faith*, II, 30.

How can eating fruit act have produced such catastrophic results? It is because Adam and Eve had no possible excuse for their disobedience. They lacked nothing, being already possessed of what is most valuable — that is, communion with God. All possible appetites of the body and spirit were satisfied and they had no bad habits or dispositions to incline them to evil. Therefore in this one act they voluntarily separated themselves from Good and aligned themselves with evil. They became partakers of Satan's downfall, yet not wholly evil as those demons were. Bishop Ignatius Brianchaninov wrote in 1867 that man's

> fall, on account of the way in which it took place, assumed quite a different character from that of the angels. The angels fell consciously, deliberately, intentionally; they themselves were the cause of the evil within them. Having committed one transgression, they madly rushed to another. For these reasons they were completely deprived of good, were filled to overflowing with evil, and have only evil as their nature. Man fell unconsciously, unintentionally; he was deceived and seduced. For this reason his natural goodness was not destroyed, but was mixed with the evil of the fallen angels. But this natural goodness, being mixed with evil, poisoned with evil, became worthless, inadequate, unworthy of God Who is perfect, purest goodness. Man for the most part does evil, meaning to do good, not seeing the evil

wrapped in a mask of goodness on account of the darkening of his mind and conscience. The fallen spirits do evil for the sake of evil, finding enjoyment and fame in doing evil.[41]

At the instant of mankind's sin, death came into the world—that which we call the "first death" to distinguish it from the second death which is eternal.

Thus, in soul Adam died immediately, as soon as he had tasted; and later, after nine hundred and thirty years, he died also in body. For, as the death of the body is the separation from it of the soul, so the death of the soul is the separation from it of the Holy Spirit. Later, for this reason, the whole human race also became such as our forefather Adam became through the fall--mortal, that is, both in soul and body. Man such as God created him no longer existed in the world. And there was no possibility that anyone should become such as Adam was before the transgression of the commandment. But it was necessary that there should be such a man.[42]

The "natural" order of things as they are now is not according to the original divine plan. That living things are born and die—all this proceeded from mankind's fall from grace, as John of Damascus writes:

---

[41] Bishop Ignatius Brianchaninov, *The Arena*, p. 186.
[42] Symeon the New Theologian, *The First Created Man*, p. 45.

For the origin of all things is from God, but their destruction has been introduced by our wickedness for our punishment or benefit. For God did not create death, neither does He take delight in the destruction of living things. But death is the work rather of man, that is, its origin is in Adam's transgression, in like manner as all other punishments.[43]

The Two Brothers

There is something of sibling rivalry in this situation, and it is by no means difficult to conceive the angels as cosmic brothers of men. St. Cyril of Jerusalem intimates this sibling struggle between men and angels when he says, "For as He took the unbrotherly purpose of Joseph's brethren for a groundwork of His own dispensation, and, by permitting them to sell their brother from hatred, so he permitted the devil to wrestle, that the victors might be crowned."

Jesus also illustrated a dynamic between two brothers in parables. Consider the parable of the prodigal son, for example. Commentators on this parable typically focus attention on the younger brother, since he obviously represents mankind. But what of the older brother, who is ever with God and never transgresses His commandment? As this description could apply to no human, it very well may indicate the elder brethren

---

[43] John of Damascus, *An Exact Exposition of the Orthodox Faith,* II, 28.

of the angelic host, who have always been faithful to God. And, though the parable ends before we learn how the elder brother responded to the father's entreaties, we may assume that he overcame his anger, joined in the welcoming feast, and thereafter helped the younger brother find his place again in the heavenly household.

Another of the Lord's parables describes two brothers, yet the implications of the story are vastly different:

> A certain man had two sons; and he came to the first, and said, Son, go work to day in my vineyard. He answered and said, I will not: but afterward he repented, and went. And he came to the second, and said likewise. And he answered and said, I go, sir: and went not. (Mat. 21:28-30).

As in the previous parable, the story begins by describing a son who refuses to share in the labors of the household. He will not work—he prefers his own will to his father's will. We are not told whether he demands his share of the inheritance then suffers the consequences of immoderate living—although it is reasonable to assume all this. What we *do* know is that he ultimately repents and willingly does as his father asks. In this he fully represents mankind, which is capable of sorrow and contrition.

However, this son's brother has a very different character from the elder brother of the first parable. Three aspects are salient about him: First, he is a liar, for he says, "I go" when he is in fact not going. Second, he is disobedient, for he does not do what his father asks. Third, he is impenitent, for he never has a change of heart—or so the parable leads us to assume.

The (presumably younger) brother of this parable was, by contrast, not dishonest. Second, his disobedience was temporary, and third, it was redeemed by repentance. And of course, the elder brother of the previous parable was never dishonest or disobedient. Therefore, if we are at all justified in seeing mankind in the figure of this younger brother, then the elder brother must represent not faithful and obedient angels, but fallen, disobedient ones. These two stories offer some idea of the intensity of the heavenly dynamic surrounding angels and men.

Man's Angelic Destiny

It should never be forgotten that man was created to abide in heaven and that someday this will be his eternal experience. Since God intends man to fill the places in heaven vacated by the fallen angels, someday that will happen—but when? These momentous happenings at the dawn of time are linked to what shall be at the conclusion of time and the end of the world, for the Lord's return and judgment is said to hinge on heaven's empty ranks being filled by Christian believers. According to Elder Lavrenty, a nineteenth century Russian monastic and visionary,

> Until the number of fallen angels is restored, the Lord will not come to judge. But in the last

time [i.e., at the very end] the Lord will add to the number of angels from those living who are written in the Book of Life, in order to make up the number of the fallen.[44]

The Apostles and fathers left no doubt that man's eternal destiny was sure, and that, in the fullness of time the "righteous in heaven will be like the angels of God" (Mark 12:25). Then the "thousands of angels will receive men into their midst as brothers, and will share with them their feelings of love and thanksgiving towards God (Heb. 12:22, 23)."[45]

The Lord emphasized that the first would be last and the last first. So it is that the primal state of innocence which mankind enjoyed in God's company will eventually be realized again, but on a higher and more spiritually mature level. "Such was the first creation, and such will be the restoration after this," says St. Basil. "Man will return to his ancient constitution in rejecting malice, a life weighed down with cares, the slavery of the soul with regard to daily worries. When he has renounced all this, he will return to that paradisal life which was not enslaved to the passions of the flesh, which is free, the life of closeness to God, a partaker of the life of the angels."[46]

---

[44] Schema-Archimandrite Lavrenty of the Chernigov-Trinity Convent, "The Prophetic Gift: Spiritual Heroes of the Twentieth Century," translated and condensed from *Nadezhda*, no. 14, pp. 298-304.

[45] *Apostasy and Antichrist* (Jordanville, NY: Holy Trinity Monastery, 1978), p. 45.

[46] Basil the Great, *On the Origin of Man*, 2:6-7.

CHAPTER THREE

The Strong Man's House

One of Bishop Kallistos Ware's amusing and instructive anecdotes depicts three aspiring devils about to be unleashed upon the world. In order to verify that these fallen angels had received adequate training in the infernal arts, a chief demon was interrogating them.

The chief demon looked at the first devil and asked, "How will you tempt the sons of Adam when you are sent to earth?"

"I will tell them there is no God!" this devil replied with unconcealed pride.

"Hmm," muttered the chief demon morosely. "That's already been tried. Unfortunately, too many people know Him personally."

After grinding his teeth in vexation for several moments, the chief demon turned to the second devil. "How will you tempt the sons of Adam when you are sent to earth?" he growled.

"I will tell them there is no devil!" the ugly thing boasted.

"That is more ingenious at least," said the demon with a sigh. "The trouble is, most of them are already living in their own hell."

The chief demon then wailed and beat his fists together with extraordinary vigor. When at last the violence of his twisted emotions was somewhat spent, he cast a wary glance at the third devil. "And how will you tempt the sons of Adam when sent to earth?" he inquired suspiciously.

This devil's cunning dark brows quivered with evil glee as he replied, "I will tell them there is no hurry!"

"Excellent!" the chief demon shrieked, his black countenance brightening by that imperceptible amount allowed to infernal beings. "Get to work!"

The devils did their job well, for mankind lost the sense of life being a temporary period in which to seek God, and of the importance of using time wisely for that purpose. Satan was strong and his influence intense. Even the first humans born on earth were immersed in tragedy—for Cain murdered his brother Abel. Sinfulness spread so rapidly that before long it had inundated the earth and God decided to cleanse the planet. All people except for the handful surrounding Noah were exterminated in the great Flood. After Noah's descendants began to repopulate the earth, again the Evil One deceived them until virtually all of them believed in idols and heathen deities. Then God selected Abraham and through him reserved to Himself a small group of people, the Israelites. Sadly, even with all the blessings and miraculous interventions bestowed on the Jews, they also were unfaithful to God.

Why was it so difficult for mankind to live virtuously, as he had been created to do? This was largely because of the influence of Satan. For, after Lucifer through the serpent had tempted Eve and caused the first humans to sin, God cursed this angel and he became from that time forward evil: "After the fall of the first created people, the tempter Lucifer was cursed by God and became absolute Evil, the Devil, Satan."[47]

The very word "Satan" indicates his character as a serpent in opposition to God, as Justin Martyr explains:

> For "Sata" in the Jewish and Syrian tongue means apostate; and "Nas" is the word from which he is called by interpretation the *serpent*, i.e., according to the interpretation of the Hebrew term, from both of which there arises the single word *Satanas*.[48]

Prince of the Power of the Air

Lucifer brought about Eve's demise not through force, but rather deception — by lying and manipulating her thoughts. Even so, Satan continues to deceive by means of lies and manipulating minds. Metaphysically speaking, mentality is considered to be an "air" aspect, and in that sense the air is Satan's domain. St. Paul points out, "In time past ye walked according to the course of the world, according to the prince of the power of the air, the spirit that now worketh in the children of disobedience" (Eph. 2:2).

Augustine pessimistically opines, "The life of demons and men, the one in the air, the other on earth, is filled with misery, calamities, and mistakes."[49] It is important to note that, according to Christian

---

[47] Bishop Nektary, p. 315.
[48] Justin Martyr, "Dialogue with Trypho," p. 251.
[49] Augustine, *City of God*, XX, 1.

understanding, devils do not exert their influence underground, as some folk tales teach, but rather in the air—the realm of mind.

The world of the carnal mind, then, is Satan's realm in which he reigns. The devil's domain is also called his "house." Here he is a strong man in control of the premises, and from this vantage point he has influenced humanity to follow his own path of rebellion. "The primordial enemy of man—the devil—is constantly at work to divert us from the Way, and he does this by making suggestions to us in the form of thoughts," says Hieromonk Damascene.[50]

From the moment of Adam and Eve's disobedience, Satan had gained a strategic foothold in their minds. Mankind's parents acquired, as the serpent had correctly said, knowledge not only of good, but also of evil. And as their children spread throughout the earth, the knowledge of evil—under Satan's influence—grew much more than the knowledge of good. Gradually the consciousness of good, or God, was forgotten and their minds became increasingly base and carnal, as St. Paul says: "As they did not like to retain God in their knowledge, God gave them over to a reprobate mind" (Rom. 1:27).

Disobedience and Death

The experience of humanity during those times was one of misery. Cast out from the Garden of Eden, they

---

[50] Damascene (Christensen), p. 311.

were compelled to labor in body for sustenance. Meanwhile they were subject always to the temptations of Satan oppressing their minds. St. Symeon the New Theologian describes their loss: "God banished them from Paradise, as from a royal palace, to live in the world as exiles. At that time also He decreed that a flaming sword should be turned and should guard the entrance into Paradise. And God did not curse Paradise, since it was the image of the future unending life of the eternal Kingdom of Heaven, but cursed only the rest of the earth, which was also incorrupt and brought forth everything by itself; and this was in order that Adam might not have any longer a life free from exhausting labors and sweat."[51]

But the chief misery was, perhaps, not the physical labors, nor even the mental labors, but the inclination within their own souls to disobey God. Their punishment for willfully disobeying God was that they willfully continued to disobey, and thus to remove themselves ever further from communion with Him who is the source of all peace and good.

> What but disobedience was the punishment of
> disobedience in that sin? For what else is man's
> misery but his own disobedience to himself, so
> that in consequence of his not being willing to
> do what he could do, he now wills to do what
> he cannot? For in spite of himself his mind is

[51] St. Symeon the New Theologian, *The First Created Man*, p. 91.

frequently disturbed, and his flesh suffers, and grows old, and dies.[52]

The disobedience of Adam and Eve created such a gulf between humanity and God that not even the most righteous person could be saved. All died and went to *Sheol*, also called Hades. "After the transgression of Adam no one even among the righteous could be saved, since all men were subject to the sin of the fore-father Adam, to corruption and death, and the fiery sword allowed no one into the Paradise from which Adam had been banished."[53]

From this condition there was no escape. The first death, that of the body, led inexorably to the second death, that of the soul. Mankind's condition was hope-less. "By them so great a sin was committed, that by it the human nature was altered for the worse, and was transmitted also to their posterity, liable to sin and subject to death," declared Augustine. "And the king-dom of death so reigned over men, that the deserved penalty for sin would have hurled all headlong even into the second death, of which there is no end, had not the undeserved grace of God saved some therefrom."[54]

Enter the Thief

But the undeserved grace of God accomplished its ends in a surprising way. Not as a king did Jesus Christ

---

[52] Augustine, *City of God*, p. 46.
[53] Symeon the New Theologian, *The First Created Man*, p. 73.
[54] Augustine, *City of God*, p. 441.

appear to men, but as a servant. Not in triumph, as the world thinks of triumph, but in the failure of death. Not in honor, but in the disgrace of a lawbreaker.

To the unsaved, Jesus was a criminal. "If he were not a malefactor we would not have delivered him up unto thee," shouted the Jews to Pilate (John 18:30). And Isaiah prophesied, "He was numbered among the transgressors" (Is. 53:12). Even Jesus characterized Himself as a robber. "Are ye come out as against a thief with swords and staves for to take me?" He asked His accusers (Mat. 26:55). And to His own disciples He said, "If therefore thou shalt not watch, I will come on thee as a thief, and thou shalt not know what hour I will dome upon thee" (Rev. 3:3).

A thief enters a house silently and unsuspected in order to steal what is valuable. And it is in this capacity that the Lord vandalized the house or domain of Satan, whom He calls, ironically, the good man. "And this know, that if the good man of the house had known what hour the thief would come, he would have watched, and not have suffered his house to be broken through" (Luke 12:39).

Since not even the angels know the hour of the Lord's coming, Satan, being a fallen angel, was tricked. The Lord revealed that, in binding the "strong man," He would be able to freely steal the strong man's possessions from his house: "How can one enter into a strong man's house, and spoil his goods, except he bind the strong man? And then he will spoil his house." (Mat. 12:29).

The Strong Man

We are not to misunderstand the identity of the strong man, and Augustine asserts that the Lord is

> meaning by the strong man the devil, because he had power to take captive the human race; and meaning by his goods which he was to take, those who had been held by the devil in diverse sins and iniquities, but who were to become believers in Himself.[55]

Lest there be any question whether Satan had such power, the Scripture records his own words when tempting Jesus:

> And the devil, taking him up into an high mountain, showed him all the kingdoms of the world in a moment of time. And the devil said unto him, all this power will I give thee, and the glory of them: for that is delivered unto me; and to whomsoever I will I give it (Luke 4:5-6).

Yet we should not suppose that Christ approached Satan as a thief from a position of weakness. Satan is strong, but Christ is stronger. "When a strong man armed keepeth his palace, his goods are in peace: But when a stronger than he shall come upon him, and overcome him, he taketh away from him all his armor wherein he trusted, and divideth his spoils. He that is not with me is against me: and he that gathereth not with me scattereth" (Luke 11:21-23). Here we sense that

[55] Augustine, *City of God*, XX, 7.

"he that is not with me" definitely refers to Satan. A similar statement in Mark makes it clear that one cannot be a fence straddler with regard to God: "There is no man which shall do a miracle in my name, that can lightly speak evil of me. For he that is not against us is on our part" (Mark 9:39-40).

From that time forward, Satan lost his dominating influence over men's minds. His house was spoiled and he was no longer all-powerful in the mental realm in which he had reigned supreme. Perhaps speaking of this, and using the word heaven to refer to the airy sphere of the devil, Jesus says, "I beheld Satan as lightning fall from heaven" (Luke 10:18).

It is worth noting that Christ's second coming will be witnessed first in Satan's realm of air, that by this we may know the evil one is permanently conquered: "For as the lightning cometh out of the east, and shineth even unto the west; so shall also the coming of the Son of man be" (Mat. 24:27). Similarly, on the personal level it is in the realm of mind that Christ first overcomes Satan in each of us: "Be ye transformed by the renewing of your mind" (Rom. 12:2), and "Let this mind be in you, which was also in Christ Jesus" (Phil. 2:5).

Bound by the Resurrection

Satan's binding is traditionally depicted in the icon of Christ's resurrection. Here the Lord stands above the gates of hell, broken by the force of His exit. In each hand he holds the wrists of Adam and Eve, the first of the Satan's "goods" to be spoiled. Christ is snatching them away from the devil's kingdom of sin and death, and not only them, but also all the righteous who lived before His coming. Beneath the feet of the risen Lord lies the black figure of Satan in a very humiliated posture. He is bound with chains, and writhes the darkness of his despoiled palace. St. John writes:

> I saw an angel come down from heaven, having the key of the abyss, and a chain in his hand. And he held the dragon, that old serpent, which is called the Devil and Satan, and bound him for a thousand years, and cast him into the abyss, and shut him up, and set a seal upon him, that he should deceive the nations no more, till the thousand years should be finished: after this he must be loosed a little season (Rev. 20: 1-3).

This scene from Revelation is a description of the strong man being bound so Christ could spoil his goods:

> It was then for the binding of this strong one that the apostle saw in the Apocalypse "an angel coming down from heaven, having the key of the abyss, and a chain in his hand. And he laid hold," he says, "on the dragon, that old serpent, which is called the devil and Satan, and bound him a thousand years," — that is, bridled and restrained his power so that he

could not seduce and gain possession of those who were to be freed.[56]

That the devil is bound, and cast into the abyss, and shut up, means that he is restricted in the full exercise of his ability to corrupt and tempt mankind. From the time of our Lord's first coming, Christ's Church is formed where the Gospel is preached. Men are summoned to the kingdom of God, and the devil is barred from preventing their entrance into it. According to Victorinus, "'He shut the door upon him,' it is said, that is, he forbade and restrained his seducing those who belong to Christ."[57]

The Devil in Duress

But why were such measures needed against Satan? As Christ's life revealed more of mankind's divine potential, it also revealed more of the punishment laid up for the devil. Justin Martyr writes that although Satan had continually been devising temptations for humanity, he was not fully aware of his own doom:

> But when the Lord appeared, and the devil clearly understood that eternal fire was laid up and prepared for him and his angels, he then began to plot without ceasing against the faithful, being desirous to have many companions in his apostasy, that he might not by himself

---

[56] Augustine, *City of God*, XX, 7.
[57] Victorinus, *Commentary on the Apocalypse of the Blessed John*, XX.

endure the shame of condemnation, comforting himself by this cold and malicious consolation.[58]

Therefore, except the Lord had forcefully bound Satan, it might be that the world would have again become steeped in absolute evil in which none could be saved. Augustine writes:

> The binding of the devil is his being prevented from the exercise of his whole power to seduce men, either by violently forcing or fraudulently deceiving them into taking part with him. If he were during so long a period permitted to assail the weakness of men, very many persons, such as God would not wish to expose to such temptation, would have their faith overthrown, or would be prevented from believing; and that this might not happen, he is bound.[59]

Meanwhile, the abyss into which Satan is cast refers to the hearts of those who have already rejected God. And this explains how it can be that even with the devil bound and the Church growing, there remains an excess of evil in the world until the consummation. "The devil," writes Victorinus, "excluded from the hearts of believers, began to take possession of the wicked, in whose hearts, blinded day by day, he is shut up as if in a profound abyss."[60]

---

[58] Justin Martyr, Fragments of lost writings, *The Ante-Nicene Fathers*, vol. 1, p. 300.

[59] Augustine, *City of God*, XX, 8.

[60] Victorinus, *Commentary on the Apocalypse of the Blessed John*, XX.

In being restricted from influencing believers, the devil affects even more those who have already sided with him: "By the abyss is meant the countless multitude of the wicked whose hearts are unfathomably deep in malignity against the Church of God," says Augustine. "Not that the devil was not there before, but he is said to be cast in thither, because, when prevented from harming believers, he takes more complete possession of the ungodly."[61]

I Come Quickly

According to the Bible, forty-two generations elapsed from Abraham to Jesus Christ, during which time Satan's influence upon mankind grew stronger and stronger. It might well be asked, why did God delay so long in sending help?

One answer is that the evil latent in mankind had to increase enough to produce outward manifestations before it could be appropriately healed. According to Gregory of Nyssa,

> In diseases, for instance, of the body, when some corrupt humour spreads unseen beneath the pores, before all the unhealthy secretion has been detected on the skin, they who treat diseases by the rules of art do not use such medicines as would harden the flesh, but they wait till all that lurks within comes out upon the surface, and then, with the disease un-

[61] Augustine, *City of God*, XX, 7.

masked, apply their remedies... For this reason it was that He did not produce his healing for man's disease immediately on Cain's hatred and murder of his brother; for the wickedness of those who were destroyed in the days of Noah had not yet burst into a flame, nor had that terrible disease of Sodomite lawlessness been displayed, nor the Egyptians' war against God, nor the pride of Assyria, nor the Jews' bloody persecution of God's saints, nor Herod's cruel murder of the children, nor whatever else is recorded, or if unrecorded was done in the generations that followed, the root of evil budding forth in divers manners in the willful purposes of man. When, then, wickedness had reached its utmost height, and there was no form of wickedness which men had not dared to do, to the end that the healing remedy might pervade the whole of the diseased system, He, accordingly, ministers to the disease; not at its beginning, but when it had been completely developed."[62]

---

[62] Gregory of Nyssa, *The Great Catechism*, XXIX.

CHAPTER FOUR

The New Israel

One of history's most perplexing facts is that the people upon whom God lavished many blessings in order to prepare them for receiving the greatest blessing of His only begotten Son, turned their backs on Him. We will not attempt in these few pages to adequately examine the complex record of God's promises to and forbearance with hard-hearted Israel, as that would be a book in itself. Nevertheless it is useful to get a perspective on how Israel and the Church are related.

Our Lord pined over the lost sheep of the house of Israel, and lamented,

> O Jerusalem, Jerusalem, thou that killest the prophets, and stonest them which are sent unto thee, how often would I have gathered they children together, even as a hen gathereth her chickens under her wings, and ye would not! Behold, your house is left unto you desolate. For I say unto you, ye shall not see me henceforth, till ye shall say, blessed is he that cometh in the name of the Lord (Mat. 23:37-38).

It is curious that this is the only instance in the entire Bible in which either hens or chickens are mentioned. Perhaps by this unique analogy Jesus revealed the exclusive care He wished to bestow upon the

Jews. One cannot help but wonder what course history might have taken if they had at that time recognized their Messiah. Jesus said often that the first would be last and the last first. It is certainly reasonable to assume that Israel is counted in the category of "first," for the Jews clearly received priority in God's reckoning. St. John Chrysostom points out what care Jesus took that the Jews might receive every opportunity to repent and be saved:

> He said to them, "Go ye and make disciples of all nations." We would say, that both before the crucifixion, and after the crucifixion, they [the apostles] addressed themselves to them [Jews] first. For both before the crucifixion, He saith to them, "Go to the lost sheep of the house of Israel;" and after the crucifixion, so far from forbidding, He even commanded them to address themselves to the Jews. For though He said, "Make disciples of all nations," yet when on the point of ascending into Heaven, He declared that unto those first they were to address themselves.[63]

The Lost Sheep of the House of Israel

The Jews were uppermost in our Lord's thoughts, and He acknowledged being sent to them alone. "I am not sent but unto the lost sheep of the house of Israel"

---

[63] John Chrysostom, *Homilies on the Gospel According to Matthew*, LXIX.

(Mat. 15:24). He tells His disciples not to go to the house of Israel, but to the lost sheep of the house of Israel (although by this He may have meant the entire group).

When those for whom the Gospel is intended refuse to hear, that wondrous message is preached to others east and west. It is they who will join the patriarchs in heavenly places: "Many shall come from the east and west, and shall sit down with Abraham, and Isaac, and Jacob, in the kingdom of heaven. But the children of the kingdom shall be cast out into outer darkness: there shall be weeping and gnashing of teeth" (Mat. 8:11). Who are the children of the kingdom if not those lost sheep of the house of Israel to whom Jesus was sent?

And what is this outer darkness that the Lord warned against? What is this place of weeping and gnashing of teeth? It is hell itself, as He makes clear later in denouncing the scribes and Pharisees: "Woe unto you, scribes and Pharisees, hypocrites! Ye serpents, ye generation of vipers, how can ye escape the damnation of hell?" (Mat. 23:27, 33).

Parables

Jesus showed by means of his parables how the Jews had failed to love God, and what was to happen on account of that.

> There was a certain householder, which planted a vineyard, and hedged it round about, and digged a winepress in it, and built a tower, and let it out to husbandmen, and went into a far country. And when the time of the fruit drew

near, he sent his servants to the husbandmen, that they might receive the fruits of it. And the husbandmen took his servants, and beat one, and killed another, and stoned another. Again, he sent other servants more than the first: and they did unto them likewise. But last of all he sent unto them his son, saying, they will reverence my son. But when the husbandmen saw the son, they said among themselves, this is the heir; come, let us kill him, and let us seize on his inheritance. And they caught him, and cast him out of the vineyard, and slew him. When the lord therefore of the vineyard cometh, what will he do unto those husbandmen? They say unto him, he will miserably destroy those wicked men, and will let out his vineyard unto other husbandmen, which shall render him the fruits in their seasons. Jesus saith unto them, did ye never read in the scriptures, the stone which the builders rejected, the same is become the head of the corner; this is the Lord's doing, and it is marvelous in our eyes? Therefore I say unto you, the kingdom of God shall be taken from you, and given to a nation bringing forth the fruits thereof (Mat. 21:33-43).

They had rejected God's messengers, the prophets, and even killed His son. The result of this is that the kingdom of God, for which they should have been prepared, was to be given instead to the Gentiles. Another parable describes the situation in terms of a wedding to whom the favored guests would not go:

> The kingdom of heaven is like unto a certain king, which made a marriage for his son, and sent forth his servants to call them that were bidden to the wedding: and they would not come. Again, he sent forth other servants, saying, Tell them which are bidden, behold, I have prepared my dinner: my oxen and my fatlings are killed, and all things are ready: come unto the marriage. But they made light of it, and went their ways, one to his farm, another to his merchandise: and the remnant took his servants, and entreated them spitefully, and slew them. But when the king heard thereof, he was wroth: and he sent forth his armies, and destroyed those murderers, and burned up their city. Then saith he to his servants, the wedding is ready, but they which were bidden were not worthy. Go ye therefore into the highways, and as many as ye shall find, bid to the marriage. So those servants went out into the highways, and gathered together as many as they found, both bad and good: and the wedding was furnished with guests (Mat. 22:1-10).

Here we see that, again, the blessing would go not to those for whom it was prepared, but to virtual bystanders. Those who had been invited were aware of their favored position and permitted themselves conceits of ingratitude. The bystanders, on the other hand, could scarce believe the good fortune in coming into a place for which nothing but grace could have gained them entrance.

St. John Chrysostom considers this parable, and the one preceding it, definitive in outlining the Jews' fate:

This parable proclaims beforehand both the casting out of the Jews, and the calling of the Gentiles; and it indicates together with this also the strictness of the life required, and how great the punishment appointed for the careless. And well is this placed after the other. For He had said, "It shall be given to a nation bringing forth the fruits thereof." What then could be more ungrateful than they, when being bidden to a marriage they rush away? For who would not choose to come to a marriage, and that a King's marriage, and of a King making a marriage for a Son? What then did He after these things? Since they were not willing to come, yea and also slew those that came unto them; He burns up their cities, and sent His armies and slew them. See then care unutterable. He had planted a vineyard; He had done all things, and finished; when His servants had been put to death, He sent other servants; when those had been slain, He sent the son; and when He was put to death, He bids them to the marriage. They would not come, after this He sends other servants, and they slew these also. Then upon this He slays them, as being incurably diseased.

For that they were incurably diseased, was proved not by their acts only, but by the fact, that even when harlots and publicans had believed, they did these things. So that, not by their own crimes alone, but also from what others were able to do aright, these men are condemned. Therefore Christ also saith, "The wedding is ready, but they which were bidden were not worthy."[64]

A Failure of Faith

The catastrophe of the Jews comes down to a failure of faith. For over and over as Jesus preached and ministered in Judea, he encountered those who would not believe. "I have not found so great faith, no, not in Israel" said the Lord after healing the centurion's servant (Mat. 8:10). And both of these were certainly Gentiles. "Thy faith hath saved thee" (Luke 18:42) said Jesus, and St. Paul echoes these words, "By grace are ye saved through faith" (Eph. 2:8). As it is not possible to be saved without faith, what fate awaits the Jews?

"It is not without reason that the Lord Himself says to the Jews, 'Had ye believed Moses, ye would have believed me; for he wrote of me,'" wrote Augustine.

For by receiving the law carnally without perceiving that its earthly promises were figures of things spiritual, they fell into such murmurings

---

[64] John Chrysostom, *Homilies on the Gospel According to Matthew*, LXIX.

as audaciously to say, "It is vain to serve God; and what profit is it that we have kept His ordinance, and that we have walked suppliantly before the face of the Lord Almighty? And now we call aliens happy; yea, they that work wickedness are set up."[65]

Israel Divorced

Old Testament prophets sometimes characterized Israel as an unfaithful wife. "Surely as a wife treacherously departeth from her husband, so have ye dealt treacherously with me, O house of Israel, saith the Lord" (Jer. 3:20). Here again, faith is what Israel lacks — not expressed as the faith of belief, but rather the faith of loyalty and fidelity. Origen describes the situation in terms that make the estrangement appear permanent, for, because the wife has been faithless, the longsuffering husband finally gives her a bill of divorcement. This leaves Him free to seek a more faithful bride:

> The mother of the people separated herself from Christ, her husband, without having received the bill of divorcement, but afterwards when there was found in her an unseemly thing, and she did not find favor in his sight, the bill of divorcement was written out for her; for when the new covenant called those of the Gentiles to the house of Him who had cast

[65] Augustine, *City of God*, XX, 28

away his former wife, it virtually gave the bill of divorcement to her who formerly separated from her husband — the law, and the Word.[66]

The New Bride of Christ

The joyful event toward which all sacred history inclines is the marriage of the Lamb. "Let us be glad and rejoice, and give honour to him: for the marriage of the Lamb is come, and his wife hath made herself ready. And he saith unto me, Write, Blessed are they which are called unto the marriage" (Rev. 19:7).

Faithful believers are invited to this great wedding, even as the Jews had once been. They are expected to be watching for it: "Let your loins be girded about, and your lights burning; and ye yourselves like unto men that wait for their lord, when he will return from the wedding: that when he cometh and knocketh, they may open unto him immediately" (Luke 12:35-36).

The parable of the ten virgins also takes place at a wedding. The wise virgins were prepared and thus were able to go into the wedding feast, while the foolish virgins were not: "the bridegroom came; and they that were ready went in with him to the marriage: and the door was shut" (Mat. 25:11).

Who is this lucky person, this pure bride, the Lamb of God is marrying? St. John the Theologian describes her as a city — the heavenly Jerusalem. "And I John saw the holy city, New Jerusalem, coming down from God

[66] Origen, *Commentary on Matthew*, XIV, 19.

out of heaven, prepared as a bride adorned for her husband" (Rev. 21:2).

St. Paul used the analogy of husband and wife to describe the relationship of Christ with His church, the assembly of all those souls who believe in Him: "For this cause shall a man leave his father and mother, and shall be joined unto his wife, and they two shall be one flesh. This is a great mystery: but I speak concerning Christ and the church" (Eph. 5:31-32).

And yet, the marriage of two humans only approximates the depth of intertwining communion existing between the Lord and His Church. For they become, as it were, one flesh and one body. "For the husband is head of the wife, even as Christ is the head of the church: and he is the saviour of the body" (Eph. 5:23).

The Children of Abraham

Genealogy was an important matter for the Jews, as was proof of their descent from Abraham. Therefore these words of Jesus must have seemed revolutionary to them: "And think not to say within yourselves, we have Abraham to our father, for I say unto you, that God is able of these stones to raise up children unto Abraham" (Mat. 3:9). Irenaeus believed that the children which God raised up as descendents of Abraham were in fact Christians: "The church is the seed of Abraham; and for this reason, that we may know that He who in the New Testament 'raises up stones unto Abraham' is He who will gather, according to the Old

74

Testament, those that shall be saved from all the nations."[67]

Does all this mean that Israel has no further part to play in the sacred drama, and no expectation of God's mercy? Not according to St. Paul, who explained at length that Israel's stubbornness benefited the Gentiles, and that the blindness of the Jews led to the Lord's light being spread into the rest of the world.

"I say then, Hath God cast away his people? God forbid. For I also am an Israelite, of the seed of Abraham, *of* the tribe of Benjamin. God hath not cast away his people which he foreknew. Wot ye not what the scripture saith of Elias? how he maketh intercession to God against Israel, saying, Lord, they have killed thy prophets, and digged down thine altars; and I am left alone, and they seek my life. But what saith the answer of God unto him? I have reserved to myself seven thousand men, who have not bowed the knee to *the image of* Baal. Even so then at this present time also there is a remnant according to the election of grace... As concerning the gospel, *they are* enemies for your sakes: but as touching the election, *they are* beloved for the fathers' sakes. For the gifts and calling of God *are* without repentance. For as ye in times past have not believed God, yet have now obtained mercy through their unbelief: Even so have these also now not believed, that through your mercy they also may obtain mercy. For God hath concluded them all in unbelief, that he might have mercy upon all." (Rom. 11:1-32).

[67] Irenaeus, *Against Heresies*, 5:34:1.

The Repentance of Israel

This national conversion of the remnant of the Jewish faith is prophesied to occur in the last days at the instigation of two miraculous men, Elias and Enoch, both of whom were previously taken up into heaven alive.

> It is a familiar theme in the conversation and heart of the faithful that in the last days before the judgment the Jews shall believe in the true Christ, that is, our Christ, by means of this great and admirable prophet Elias who shall expound the law to them. For not without reason do we hope that before the coming of our Judge and Savior Elias shall come, because we have good reason to believe that he is now alive; for, as Scripture most distinctly informs us, he was taken up from this life in a chariot of fire. When, therefore, he is come, he shall give a spiritual explanation of the law which the Jews at present understand carnally, and shall thus "turn the heart of the father to the son," that is, the heart of fathers to their children; for the Septuagint translators have frequently put the singular for the plural number. And the meaning is, that the sons, that is, the Jews, shall understand the law as the fathers, that is, the prophets, and among them Moses himself, understood it."[68]

[68] Augustine, *City of God*, XX, 29.

Elias and Enoch are the two candlesticks mentioned in the Book of Revelation. "He speaks of Elias the prophet, who is the precursor of the times of Antichrist, for the restoration and establishment of the churches from the great and intolerable persecution," says Victorinus.[69]

Israel's Restoration

If the prophesies of the Old Testament are to ever come true, then it seems that Israel, or a remnant thereof, will eventually be redeemed and restored to God's favor. Isaiah waxes eloquent about that ultimate bliss which the Jews are to enjoy in God's presence:

> And there shall come forth a rod out of the stem of Jesse, and a Branch shall grow out of his roots: and the spirit of the Lord shall rest upon him, the spirit of wisdom and understanding, the spirit of counsel and might, the spirit of knowledge and of the fear of the Lord; and shall make him of quick understanding in the fear of the Lord... And righteousness shall be the girdle of his loins, and faithfulness the girdle of his reins. The wolf also shall dwell with the lamb, and the leopard shall lie down with the kid; and the calf and the young lion and the fatling together; and a little child shall lead them... And in that day there shall be a

---

[69] Victorinus, *Commentary on the Apocalypse of the Blessed John,* VII, 2.

root of Jesse, which shall stand for an ensign of the people; to it shall the Gentiles seek: and his rest shall be glorious. And it shall come to pass in that day, that the Lord shall set his hand again the second time to recover the remnant of his people" (Is. 11:1-11).

CHAPTER FIVE

The Six Ages of Mankind

Though God creates instantaneously, He does not proceed in a hurried manner. We understand from Genesis that He allowed six days for the creation of heaven and earth (Gen. 1:31-2:3). Why did not God simply make everything all at once? Since He is omnipotent, we must presume creation could have taken place thus. Perhaps He created in six days and rested on the seventh so that man, who was destined to live in time, might have these markers to guide him. For now not only the weekly cycles of the sun, but also the epochs of sacred history, keep step with the eternal cadence of the seven days of creation.

A prominent belief of the apostolic fathers was that the six days of God's creative acts would be reflected in six thousand years of history for mankind. This idea seems to be based on King David's thought: "For a thousand years in thy sight are but as yesterday when it is past, and as a watch in the night" (Psalm 90:4).

The Apostle Peter also emphasized this point in his discussing the day of judgment:

> But, beloved, be not ignorant of this one thing, that one day is with the Lord as a thousand years, and a thousand years as one day. The Lord is not slack concerning his promise, as some men count slackness; but is longsuffering

to us-ward, not willing that any should perish, but that all should come to repentance. But the day of the Lord will come as a thief in the night; in the which the heavens shall pass away with a great noise, and the elements shall melt with fervent heat, the earth also and the works that are therein shall be burned up (2 Pet. 3:8-10).

David and Peter both make the analogy of a thousand years being equivalent to one day in God's eyes, and it may reasonably be assumed that the apostle got his inspiration in the matter from his Old Testament predecessor. Early Christian writers were quick to combine these ideas with the Genesis creation account and formulate an overall plan of world history based on thousand-year periods. One of the earliest to express this is Barnabas:

> Attend, my children, to the meaning of this expression, 'He finished in six days.' This implies that the Lord will finish all things in six thousand years, for a day is with Him a thousand years... "And He rested on the seventh day." This means: when His Son, coming [again], shall destroy the time of the wicked man, and judge the ungodly, and change the-sun, and the moon, and the stars, then shall He truly rest on the seventh day."[70]

[70] *The Epistle of Barnabas.*

Irenaeus agrees with this, adding, "For in as many days as this world was made, in so many thousand years shall it be concluded."[71]

The Sixth Age

Lactantius considered that, since man was made on the sixth day of creation, he was now living through the sixth age in which man would be remade in holiness. By the conclusion of the sixth age, he believed, all wickedness would be eliminated from the earth:

> And again, since God, having finished His works, rested the seventh day and blessed it, at the end of the six thousandth year all wickedness must be abolished from the earth, and righteousness reign for a thousand years. For as, when all things were completed which were contrived for the use of man, last of all, on the sixth day, He made man also; so now on the great sixth day the true man is being formed by the word of God, that is, a holy people is fashioned for righteousness by the doctrine and precepts of God.[72]

According to this thesis, Christ's first advent signaled the beginning of mankind's sixth age, since it was on the sixth day of creation that Adam sinned and died. Irenaeus writes: "

[71] Irenaeus, *Against Heresies*, 5:28.
[72] Lactantius, *The Divine Institutes*, Book VII, XIV.

The Lord, therefore, recapitulating in Himself this day, underwent His sufferings upon the day preceding the Sabbath, that is, the sixth day of the creation, on which day man was created; thus granting him a second creation by means of His passion, which is that [creation] out of death.[73]

A Thousand Years

In Ecclesiastes we are presented with another perspective on the span of a thousand years—that of the human condition under the law and without Christ. Here the preacher complains, "Yea, though he live a thousand years twice told, yet hath he seen no good: do not all go to the one place?" (Ecc. 6:6).

Beyond this and the two references noted from Psalms and Peter's epistle, there is only one other place in the entire Bible in which a thousand years is expressed as signifying a particular thing beyond so many revolutions of the earth around the sun. In the twentieth chapter of the Book of Revelation the phrase "a thousand years" is infused with a new and dynamic meaning, one brimming with hope and possibility.

In the first seven verses of chapter 20, this phrase is used fully six times to describe a unique and unprecedented period of sacred history. Not only are we to mark the major events of this period, we are challenged to understand what they mean:

[73] Irenaeus, *Against Heresies,* V, 26.

And I saw an angel come down from heaven, having the key of the bottomless pit and a great chain in his hand. And he laid hold on the dragon, that old serpent, which is the Devil, and Satan, and bound him a thousand years. And cast him into the bottomless pit, and shut him up, and set a seal upon him, that he should deceive the nations no more, till the thousand years should be fulfilled: and after that he must be loosed a little season. And I saw thrones, and they sat upon them, and judgment was given unto them: and I saw the souls of them that were beheaded for the witness of Jesus, and for the word of God, and which had not worshiped the beast, neither his image, neither had received his mark upon their foreheads, or in their hands; and they lived and reigned with Christ a thousand years. But the rest of the dead lived not again unto the thousand years were finished. This is the first resurrection. Blessed and holy is he that hath part in the first resurrection: on such the second death hath no power, but they shall be priests of God and of Christ, and shall reign with him a thousand years. And when the thousand years are expired, Satan shall be loosed out of his prison, and shall go out to deceive the nations which are in the four quarters of the earth . . . (Rev. 20:1-7).

The Magnificent Millennium

Two primal elements of a uniquely blissful life are portrayed: First, Satan is bound and shut up where he can deceive the nations no more. Second, those who have witnessed and suffered for the sake of Jesus participate in the "first resurrection," in which they reign on thrones as priests and judges.

Given the interweaving of these two elements in Revelation 20, it is logical to assume they are contemporaneous, that is, Satan's thousand years of bondage coincides exactly with the thousand years of the saints' reign with Christ, both of them occurring at the same time. And on this point there has been general agreement throughout Christian history.

In the cosmology that had already been established to reconcile the six days of creation with six thousand years of world history, it was an easy step for early Christians to identify the thousand years of Revelation 20 with the seventh day of creation, or the expected thousand years of God's Sabbath. According to this view, strongly articulated by Lactantius and Irenaeus, the sacred reign was yet to come and would not arrive until the seventh age: "the thousand years of the kingdom, that is, seven thousand of the world."[74]

Earthly Blessedness

These writers characterized the millennium of grace as a time of earthly blessedness and prosperity, lush

---

[74] Lactantius, *The Divine Institutes*, Book VII, XXVI.

with abundance. Lactantius wrote, "and the earth will open its fruitfulness, and bring forth the most abundant fruits of its own accord; the rocky mountains shall drop with honey; streams of wine shall run down, and rivers flow with milk."[75]

From whence did Lactantius' concept come? There is nothing in the description set forth by St. John to suggest it. We read in Revelation of priests of God sitting on thrones and administering judgment—not of streams of wine and rivers of milk, still less of the revelers who would presumably be imbibing these refreshments. Even the Garden of Eden had not been portrayed in such lavish terms, for Genesis merely says "a river went out of Eden to water the garden" (Gen. 2:10), and we can assume it was a river of water.

The Sibyls Still Speak

Fortunately, one need not look far to answer this question, for Lactantius himself freely admits that his vision comes from the pre-Christian Sibyls, whose poetry he quotes approvingly:

> More brilliant than the stars, and sun and moon, hard oaks shall distil the dewy honey. Nor shall the wool learn to counterfeit various colors; but the ram himself in the meadows shall change his fleece, now for a sweetly blushing purple, now for saffron dye.[76]

---

[75] Lactantius, *The Divine Institutes*, Book VII, XXIV.
[76] Lactantius, *The Divine Institutes*, Book VII, XXIV.

It is a fantastic world indeed, in which animals are so accommodating as to change the color of their wool upon request. And Lactantius is not alone in his anticipation of such a paradise. One of the earliest apostolic fathers of whom we have written records was Papias. The fragments of Papias' writings still extant describe the future world in terms that might well be termed fabulous:

> The days will come in which vines shall grow, having each ten thousand branches, and in each branch ten thousand twigs, and in each true twig ten thousand shoots, and in every one of the shoots ten thousand clusters, and on every one of the clusters ten thousand grapes, and every grape when pressed will give five-and-twenty metres of wine. And when any one of the saints shall lay hold of a cluster, another shall cry out, "I am a better cluster, take me; bless the Lord through me"[77]

Irenaeus quotes Papias in his own work, on the authority that he was "a hearer of John and companion of Polycarp," and says that in the time of the kingdom "the creation, having been renovated and set free, shall fructify with an abundance of all kinds of food, from the dew of heaven, and from the fertility of the earth."[78]

How did such a view become popular among Christians of the second to the fourth century, espe-

[77] Fragments of Papias, *From the Exposition of the Oracles of the Lord,* IV.

[78] Irenaeus, *Against Heresies,* 5:33:3.

cially when St. Paul emphasizes, "the kingdom of God is not meat and drink" (Rom. 14:17)? St. Paul had written this to the Romans no later than A.D. 58, and was martyred shortly thereafter. The Book of Revelation, on the other hand, was composed in A.D. 95 while St. John was exiled at Patmos Island. This book, along with St. John's letters, was the last of the New Testament canon to be written.

Only in Revelations is this special millennial period mentioned — it does not appear in any gospel or epistle. Early Christian writers wanting to interpret the cryptic passages regarding the thousand years and to relate them to the doctrine of the seven ages of mankind turned to the Old Testament for corroborating ideas. There they found "gold" in the prophecies of a future time of blessing (duration unspecified) for *Israel*.

Isaac's Blessing

Irenaeus justifies his concept of an earthly paradise on the prophecies given to the Jews. In particular the blessing of Isaac, which Irenaeus says was never realized in Jacob's life, is identified with the future kingdom of abundance. Isaac had blessed Jacob with the words, "be thou lord over thy brethren" (Gen. 27:29). "The predicted blessing, therefore, belongs unquestionably to the times of the kingdom, when the righteous shall bear rule upon their rising from the dead."[79]

[79] Irenaeus, *Against Heresies*, 5:33:3.

Other prophetic writings are summoned to describe this future kingdom of abundance. The Jewish prophecies are nonetheless used to buttress the millennial vision of Irenaeus, Lactantius and others. By combining the prophecies of God's future blessing upon the Jews with the Sabbath of the Lord and the concept of seven ages of mankind, Irenaeus found a synthesis that appeared both to explain the thousand years of the Book of Revelation and to establish this period as one yet to come at some distant time.

Referring to the Lord's promise that whoever leaves brethren or parents or property for His sake shall receive an hundred fold now in this time and in the age to come eternal life, Irenaeus says,

> For what are the hundred-fold rewards in this world? These are to take place in the times of the kingdom, that is, upon the seventh day, which has been sanctified, in which God rested from all the works which He created, which is the true Sabbath of the righteous, in which they shall not be engaged in any earthly occupation; but shall have a table at hand prepared for them by God, supplying them with all sorts of dishes.[80]

How is Irenaeus justified in taking the prophetic promises made to Israel and transferring them to Christians of the millennial reign? In part at least, it is because he believes the Church to have become the co-

---

[80] Irenaeus, *Against Heresies*, 5:33:2.

inheritor of Israel's blessings: "The church is the seed of Abraham; and for this reason, that we may know that He who in the New Testament 'raises up from the stones children unto Abraham,' is He who will gather, according to the Old Testament, those that shall be saved from all the nations."[81]

Irenaeus speaks of the restoration of Abraham's inheritance and implies that this is composed only of the righteous believers in Christ. And he presents a vision in which the sacred reign of the saints follows upon the appearance and defeat of Antichrist, and the second coming of Jesus Christ. This view is commonly called Premillennialism today, meaning that the Lord is expected to return prior to the sacred millennium.

We may note in passing that, as is often the case among those who hold premillennial views, Lactantius could not forbear to anticipate a date of the Lord's return, and thought it would occur well before the year 1000 A.D.: "All expectation does not exceed the limit of two hundred years [from the time of writing]. The subject itself declares that the fall and ruin of the world will shortly take place."[82] Since millennial date setters — of whom there are too many to count — are always wrong, this necessarily calls into question not only their other conclusions, but also the very basis for interpreting the Scripture according to premillennial presuppositions.

Even premillennialists of the fourth century acknowledged that many other Christians did not agree

---

[81] Irenaeus, *Against Heresies*, 5:34:1.
[82] Lactantius, *The Divine Institutes*, Book VII, XXV.

with the idea of a millennial reign based on the Jewish prophecies. For instance, in Justin Martyr's conversation with Trypho the Jew, Trypho asked him if he really believed Jerusalem would be rebuilt and the saints would reign there. Justin replied:

> I am not so miserable a fellow, Trypho, as to say one thing and think another. I admitted to you formerly, that I and many others are of this opinion, and [believe] that such will take place, as you assuredly are aware; but, on the other hand, I signified to you that many who belong to the pure and pious faith, and are true Christians, think otherwise.[83]

The Millennium Matures

Why did they think otherwise? For one thing because the nature of the millennial kingdom as proposed by premillennialists was so material and carnal. The thousand years were to be spent on earth in the enjoyment of eating and drinking — scarcely any other activity is mentioned — the produce which the bountiful earth was to provide. The anticipation of gastronomic delights and other worldly pleasures in the wake of Christ's return so infatuated a group called the Montanists, however, that their excesses provoked a reaction in the entire Orthodox Church. In response the Second Ecumenical Council, meeting in the year 381, called

[83] Justin Martyr, *Dialog with Trypho the Jew,* LXXX.

premillennialism a superstitious aberration and admitted it to the ranks of other heresies. To affirm that the Lord's reign shall last not just one thousand years, the fathers of this council added the words "of His Kingdom there shall be no end" to the Nicene Creed.

As Christian understanding matured, the concept of Christ's millennial reign became more refined and spiritual. St. Augustine of Hippo reflected that the idea of a thousand years of rest would not be bad, were it to be a spiritual period. However, the carnality described by premillennialists calls into question their entire concept of a future millennium.

Those who have suspected that the first resurrection is future and bodily, have been moved by the number of a thousand years, as if it were a fit thing that the saints should thus enjoy a kind of Sabbath-rest during that period, a holy leisure after the labors of the six thousand years since man was created. And this opinion would not be objectionable, if it were believed that the joys of the saints in that Sabbath shall be spiritual, and consequent on the presence of God; for I myself, too, once held this opinion. But, as they assert that those who then rise again shall enjoy the leisure of immoderate carnal banquets, furnished with an amount of meat and drink such as not only to shock the feeling of the temperate, but even to pass the measure of credulity itself, such assertions can be believed only by the carnal. They who do believe them are called by name spiritual Chiliasts, which we may literally reproduce by the name Millenarians.[84]

Others joined in St. Augustine's assessment, notably Caius the Presbyter of Rome, St. Dionysios of Alexandria, Origen, Eusebius of Caesarea, St. Basil the Great, St. Gregory the Theologian, St. Epiphanius, and Blessed Jerome. And thus, a vision more in keeping with the words of Christ and the Apostles (rather than the prophets of the Old Testament) was articulated.

The Seventh Age

Since Adams' death occurred on the sixth day of creation, and Christ's death occurred figuratively on the sixth day as well, the Lord's resurrection actually marks the beginning of the seventh age. John of Damascus postulated that a full seven thousand years must elapse until the consummation—that is, until Christ's return and the Last Judgment. After this would follow an age outside the limits of time: the eighth age. By the eighth age is meant the eternal period of everlasting life in heaven.

Seven ages of this world are spoken of, that is, from the creation of the heaven and earth till the general consummation and resurrection of men. For there is a partial consummation, viz., the death of each man: but there is also a gen-

---

[84] Augustine, *The City of God*, XX, 7.

eral and complete consummation, when the general resurrection of men will come to pass. And the eighth age is the age to come. Everlasting life and everlasting punishment prove that the age or neon to come is unending. For time will not be counted by days and nights even after the resurrection, but there will rather be one day with no evening, wherein the Sun of Justice will shine brightly on the just, but for the sinful there will be night profound and limitless.[85]

The seventh age therefore indicates our present times, the period between the Lord's first and second comings, in which the Holy Spirit forms Christ's Church in the hearts of believers. After the seventh will come, according to John of Damascus, the eighth age — the unending eternal kingdom. This, succinctly, is the view passed down from apostolic and patristic sources and believed by Orthodox faithful unto this day.

[85] John of Damascus, *An Exact Exposition of the Orthodox Faith*, II, 1.

CHAPTER SIX

The Millennial Reign of Christ

A teacher once asked his students to tell him the most important moment in time and the most important place. His pupils suggested various significant historical dates. Likewise, for the most important place they put forward locations where major battles had been fought, radical discoveries made, momentous books written, and so forth.

But the teacher only shook his head solemnly at each proposed answer to his riddle. Finally the students ran out of ideas and looked to him with puzzled expressions. The most important time, he told them, is now. And the most important place is here. For only now and here can anything be done. Life happens here and now.

Man, being preoccupied with time, often thinks more of the past and the future than the present. But the present is the only time that really matters. "The truth is in the present moment," writes Hieromonk Damascene in *Christ the Eternal Tao.* "There alone do we meet our Maker, Who is Himself Truth, and lies outside our vain imaginings."[86]

---

[86] Damascene (Christensen), p. 321.

Our Lord focused mankind's attention on the present, on the here and now, by opening His public ministry with the words, "The time is fulfilled, and the kingdom of God is at hand" (Mark 1:15). The kingdom of God is at hand—it is close, not distant in either time or place. And to demonstrate that this was so, he performed wondrous acts, emphasizing that such things were proofs of the present reality of the kingdom of God: "If I cast out devils by the Spirit of God, then the kingdom of God is come unto you" (Matt. 12:28).

An Earthly Paradise

Yet, where exactly *was* this kingdom? The suspicious Jews certainly did not see it as Jesus walked the dusty roads with His ragtag disciples. They had been expecting a warrior Messiah like their forefather David to establish an earthly kingdom in which God's presence would again be with His people and all would be blessed. According to them, God's kingdom was to manifest physically upon this earth at a future time in history.

Impatient with their subservience to Rome, the Jews wanted to know when to expect this paradise of the prophets. "And when he was demanded of the Pharisees, when the kingdom of God should come, he answered them and said, the kingdom of God cometh not with observation: Neither shall they say, Lo here! or, lo there! for, behold, the kingdom of God is within you" (Luke 17:20-21). Even Jesus' disciples, who understood that He was the Anointed One but didn't yet comprehend the nature of His Kingship, asked, "Lord, wilt thou at this time restore again the kingdom to Israel?" (Acts 1:6).

Paradise Rejected

Thus, not only were the Jews unimpressed with their Messiah, they also were disappointed with the kingdom He said was at hand. For Jesus did not speak of humiliating Rome by force and establishing the Pharisees on thrones of pomp and circumstance—but rather of something invisible and apparently ineffective in the affairs of men. What could "the kingdom is within you" mean to those who would gladly rain fire and brimstone down upon Caesar's head and launch a thousand Hebrew ships against the Imperial fleet? According to their philosophy, the law of Moses was to last forever, but this upstart Jesus spoke of something new: "The law and the prophets were until John: since that time the kingdom of God is preached, and every man presseth into it" (Luke 16:16).

While the Jews believed that God's kingdom was a physical place occupying time and space, Jesus proclaimed, "My kingdom is not of this world: if my kingdom were of this world, then would my servants fight, that I should not be delivered to the Jews: but now is my kingdom not from hence" (John 18:36). The Jews believed that their position and status among men was a sign of God's favor, but Jesus preferred the world's downcast, wounded, and impoverished. "The publicans and the harlots go into the kingdom of God before you" (Matt 21:31). "Blessed be ye poor; for yours is the kingdom of God" (Luke 6:20).

Jesus had come not to destroy the law, but to fulfill it. And that fulfillment took unexpected turns; what before appeared dense and material became, at His command, refined and spiritual. Consequently, the kingdom He preached sounded worlds apart from the one that the prophets had predicted. Even the rules of the game seemed to be changing before the Jews' worried eyes: "Ye have heard that it hath been said, an eye for an eye, and a tooth for a tooth: but I say unto you, that ye resist not evil" (Mat. 5:38).

The Jew believed that whatever good could be experienced would only happen in this life, but Jesus said it was better to sacrifice anything and everything now in order to enter His kingdom in the future life: "If thine eye offend thee," He said, "pluck it out: it is better for thee to enter into the kingdom of God with one eye, than having two eyes to be cast into hell fire" (Mark 9:47).

Entering the Kingdom

The Jews had thought the kingdom would come to them, but Jesus said they must go to it. That they must *enter* it—but how? The Lord spoke of a rite of passage with both spiritual and physical (or symbolic) elements—in other words, a sacrament. "Except a man be born again, he cannot see the kingdom of God... Except a man be born of water and of the Spirit, he cannot enter into the kingdom of God" (John 3:3).

Spiritual rebirth is non-intuitive, as Nicodemus' questions demonstrated: "How can a man be born again when he is old? Can he enter the second time into his mother's womb, and be born?" (John 3:3). Yet clearly, to be reborn is to start life again at the beginning, as a baby. One entering the kingdom of God must become simple and childlike. "Suffer the little children to come to me, and forbid them not: for of such is the kingdom of God. Verily I say unto you, whosoever shall not receive the kingdom of God as a little child, he shall not enter therein" (Mark 10: 14-15).

"Art thou a master of Israel," Jesus asks Nicodemus, "and knowest not these things?" And yet, how could he know? For until the Lord died and was resurrected, all souls were bound by death. When Jesus harrowed Hell, he pulled Adam and Eve from the realm of Hades, and the good thief hanging upon the cross near Him was the first living soul to be taken to Paradise.

Before Christ's resurrection the kingdom of God was not accessible to man—not even the holiest prophets. "Among those that are born of women there is not a greater prophet than John the Baptist: but he that is least in the kingdom of God is greater than he" (Luke 7:28). Therefore as He spoke with people He could make the stunning statement, "There be some of them that stand here, which shall not taste of death, till they have seen the kingdom of God come with power" (Mark 9:1).

There were not only some, but many, who did not taste of death till they saw the kingdom of God come with power. The Apostles were the first to experience this on Pentecost, when the Holy Spirit rested upon them. The kingdom of God spread like wildfire through the world, creating children of God and believers wherever it went. St. John, writing around the year AD 90, testified that he was *in* the kingdom of God: "I John, who also am your brother, and companion in tribulation, and in the kingdom and patience of Jesus Christ, was in the isle that is called Patmos, for the word of God, and for the testimony of Jesus Christ" (Rev. 1:9).

The Kingdom of the Millennium

The Jewish vision of the kingdom as a future hope influenced several early fathers of the Church, as was noted in the last chapter. In spite of the indications by Apostles and our Lord Himself that His kingdom was a spiritual reality in the here and now, these early premillennialists adopted the Jewish model almost verbatim, only adding that this earthly paradise would be initiated by our Lord's second coming.

This teaching produced undesirable results, and it came into increasing disrepute in the early Church. Subsequently, the fathers questioned not only the nature of the millennium as described by St. John, but also its place in sacred and world history. Experience showed that the assumption of a date in some distant future led to dire excesses both in practice and in theology.

Premillennialist confusion can be witnessed in contemporary writer John Hagee's notion of the sacred millennium. He cannot make up his mind whether or not Christ's millennial reign shall be an experience of heaven on earth, due to the convoluted logistical requirements the rapture theory imposes upon reality. Hagee postulates a complex arrangement in which previously raptured (and therefore sinless?) humans will be sent back to earth during this millennium to exist shoulder to shoulder with the still sinful children of tribulation believers:

> The dispensational Age of the Kingdom, commonly known as the Millennium, will be a time of heaven on earth.... Does the Millennium sound like heaven on earth? Think again... The Millennium will be a one-thousand year lesson in man's ultimate depravity... Although Christians will live in their resurrected bodies, the Tribulation believers who go into the Millennium will bear children throughout the thousand years. The children, grandchildren, and great-grandchildren of the Millennium will possess a sinful nature, and they will have to choose whether or not to accept Christ as authority and Savor.[87]

Such disorderly concepts are not Scriptural, for premillennialists have failed to find in the gospels or epistles any definitive correlation of their views with the New Testament writings. Early attempts were made

---

[87] John Hagee, *The Revelation of Truth* (Nashville, TN: Thomas Nelson Publishers, 2000), pp. 230, 232, 250.

by Irenaeus (whose arguments subsequent premillenni-alists merely copy), but later theologians effectively disputed these.

For instance, during the Last Supper Jesus said, "I will not drink henceforth from the fruit of this vine, un-til that day when I drink it new with you in my Father's kingdom" (Luke 22:18). Irenaeus argued that by the Lord's reference to "kingdom" must be understood the future reign of grace after Christ has come again, for,

> he cannot by any means be understood as drinking of the fruit of the vine when settled down with his disciples above in a super-celestial place; nor, again, are they who drink it devoid of flesh, for to drink of that which flows from the vine pertains to flesh, and not spirit.[88]

Yet Jesus *was* with the disciples in the flesh for forty days following His resurrection. The Gospels specifi-cally record two instances of Him eating during that period, and St. John Chrysostom points out that the Lord in fact *did* drink with His disciples in order to demonstrate that He was no ghost:

> Then He saith, "I will not drink of the fruit of this wine, until that day when I drink it new with you in my Father's kingdom." And where-fore did He drink after He was risen again? Lest the grosser sort might suppose the resur-rection was an appearance. For the common sort made this an infallible test of His having

[88] Irenaeus, *Against Heresies*, Book 5:33:1.

risen again. Wherefore also the apostles also persuading them concerning the resurrection say this, "We who did eat and drink with Him."[89]

The Sacred Reign Begins

At the Last Supper, Christ Himself revealed when the sacred reign was to begin. Whenever next Jesus drinks with the disciples, He says, it will be in His Father's kingdom. After His resurrection, He does drinks with them. Therefore He is at that time *drinking in His Father's kingdom*. The millennium of grace had begun! And of course, this is the message of the Gospels—that salvation comes in the *here and now*.

The Passion of Christ thus became the fulcrum of world and sacred history, the point upon which the eons are balanced. On one arm—the past—is the beginning of everything, epitomized by God's acts of Creation; on the other arm—the future—is the end, epitomized by Glorious second coming of the Lord.

Jesus' first advent changed everything. Holiness was instituted upon the earth and Satan bound by Christ's victory. The Lord's incarnation, crucifixion, and particularly His resurrection, were the anvils upon which the Devil's chains were forged. With this understanding, the beginning of the millennium was no

---

[89] John Chrysostom, *Homilies on the Gospel of Matthew,* LXXXII, 2.

longer in question—Victorinus says that it dates from Christ's first advent and continues until His second:

> Those years wherein Satan is bound are in the first advent of Christ, even to the end of the age; and they are called a thousand, according to that mode of speaking, wherein a part is signified by the whole. He says, the thousand years should be completed, that is, what is left of the sixth day, to wit, of the sixth age.[90]

Thus, the kingdom of heaven on earth is *a present reality*. The sacred reign begins not in the distant future, but already, with the resurrection of Christ This kingdom in which the saints reign while Satan is bound is to be distinguished from the eternal kingdom to come; yet it is a foreshadowing of that blessed state says Augustine:

> But while the devil is bound, the saints reign with Christ during the same thousand years, understood in the same way, that is, of the time of His first coming. For, leaving out of account that kingdom concerning which He shall say in the end, "Come, ye blessed of my Father, take possession of the kingdom prepared for you," the Church could not now be called His kingdom or the kingdom of heaven unless His saints were even now reigning with Him, though in another and far different way; for to

---

[90] Victorinus, *Commentary on the Apocalypse of Blessed John*, XX.

His saints He says, "Lo, I am with you always, even to the end of the world."[91]

The Reign of Christ With His Saints

With the clear understanding that Christ's kingdom is here and now, the meaning of the millennium is revealed. The first element of the reign of grace is that the dragon was to be bound for a thousand years: "And I saw an angel come down from heaven, having the key of the bottomless pit and a great chain in his hand. And he laid hold on the dragon, that old serpent, which is the Devil, and Satan, and bound him a thousand years" (Rev. 20:1-2).

The second element is that believers in Christ will participate in the first resurrection and reign on thrones as priests and judges: "And I saw thrones, and them that sat upon them, and judgment was given unto them" (Rev. 20:4).

Christ's reign represents a new phase of sacred history, the period of growth of the One, Holy, Catholic and Apostolic Church, and the drawing into Christ those who would be part of His Body. Satan is bound for a figurative millennium (the Church Age), in order that those whom Christ calls might be freed from the Devil's power and respond to Him. We are to understand this "reigning" of believers as living in relationship with Christ within His Church. In describing the thrones and they who sit upon them, St. John

[91] Augustine, *The City of God*, XX, 9.

gives a symbolic picture of Christianity after the down-fall of paganism. Augustine says this is meant to show

> what the Church does or of what is done in the Church in those days. It is not to be supposed that this refers to the last judgment, but to the seats of the rulers and to the rulers themselves by whom the Church is now governed. And no better interpretation of judgment being given can be produced than that which we have in the words, "What ye bind on earth shall be bound in heaven; and what ye loose on earth shall be loosed in heaven."[92]

Bishop Averky points out that the passage refers not only to the Church Militant on earth, but the Church Triumphant in heaven, and that these are in communion:

> The holy seer of mysteries singles out in particular "those that were beheaded for the witness of Jesus and for the Word of God," that is, the holy martyrs. From this it is clear that these saints who participate in the thousand-year reign of Christ are reigning with Christ and performing judgment not on earth but in heaven, for it speaks here only concerning their souls which are not yet united with their bodies. From these words it is evident that the saints take part in the governing of the Church of Christ on earth, and therefore it is natural

[92] Augustine, *The City of God*, XX, 9.

and proper to appeal to them with prayers, asking for their intercession before Christ with whom they reign.[93]

A Definite Period of Time

In addition to a specific beginning in history, this thousand years has an equally specific historical ending (another point which the premillennial position lacks) — namely the coming of Antichrist and the Lord's return.

> St. Andrew of Caesarea interprets the passage in this way: by this "thousand years" one must understand the whole time "from the incarnation of Christ to the coming of Antichrist. With the coming of the Incarnate Son of God on earth — and in particular from the moment of His redemption of mankind through His death on the Cross — Satan was bound, paganism was cast down, and there came upon earth the thousand-year reign of Christ . . . the establishment on earth of the Church of Christ."[94]

The thousand-year reign of Christ is the seventh age that the fathers described. This is the age of God's Sabbath, beginning after the Lord's Passion — His great work — was completed. And following this is to come the eighth age. The Lord shows that this seventh age is

[93] Archbishop Averky Taushev, *The Apocalypse in the Teachings of Ancient Christianity*, (Platina, CA, St. Herman of Alaska Brotherhood, 1995), p. 253.

[94] Archbishop Averky Taushev, p. 253.

different from the eternal reign of blessedness that is to follow the end of the world by means of many parables. He describes the reign of grace as a farmer's field:

> The kingdom of heaven is likened unto a man which sowed good seed in his field. But while men slept, his enemy came and sowed tares among the wheat, and went his way. But when the blade was sprung up, and brought forth fruit, then appeared the tares also. So the servants of the householder came and said unto him, Sir, didst not thou sow good seed in thy field? From whence hath it tares? He said unto them, an enemy hath done this. The servants said unto him, Wilt thou then that we go and gather them up? But he said, Nay; lest while ye gather up the tares, ye root up also the wheat with them. Let both grow together until the harvest: and in the time of harvest I will say to the reapers, Gather ye together first the tares, and bind them in bundles to burn them: but gather the wheat into my barn (Mat. 13:24-30).

If this kingdom were the eternal one in which no evil could be present, then certainly no tares could be sown therein, which shows us that the kingdom and reign of Christ exists on this earth. This parable raises another question, namely, why could not the word of God, which is "sharper than any two edged sword, piercing even to the dividing asunder of soul and spirit," (Heb. 4:12) direct his angels to remove the tares from the field prior to the harvest? The answer lies in that realm of free will discussed earlier, which provides that no soul is destined to be either a good seed or a tare, but must so decide and live for itself. In other words, it is not clear before the harvest which plants are truly the wheat, and which the tares. A seedling may at first appear to be one, and eventually become the other. God waits patiently upon the maturing of the grain, in which each human soul draws to itself the judgment it has freely chosen.

The Lord goes on to say, "Whosoever shall break one of these least commandments, and shall teach men so, he shall be called least in the kingdom of heaven" (Mat. 5:19). But this kingdom of heaven to which the Lord refers cannot be the eternal kingdom, for otherwise this person breaking the commandments and teaching others to do so would not be in it at all. He speaks here rather of the kingdom now, when both tares and wheat exist together in the Church.

Augustine also asks this question, and provides a timeless answer:

> But in what sense are those in the kingdom of Christ who yet seek their own things in it and not the things that are Christ's? For certainly there be few who, though belonging to God's kingdom in this life, are able to mind only the things which be of God. And he answers that this kingdom is a battlefield of wars against the passions, and one in which all swords shall eventually be beaten into plows: "It is then of this kingdom militant, in which conflict with

the enemy is still maintained, and war carried on with warring lusts, or government laid upon them as they yield, until we come to that most peaceful kingdom in which we shall reign without an enemy, and it is of this first resurrection in the present life, that the Apocalypse speaks.[95].

Post millennialism

A major objective of this book is to point out how Orthodoxy differs from modern premillennialism. However there is another doctrine, commonly called postmillennialism, of which readers should be equally aware. Postmillennialism, like Orthodoxy, holds that Christ will return after the millennial reign is over.

Yet, here the similarities end. For postmillennialists believe that during this present millennium the world will become better and better until it has achieved perfection. Against this position Orthodox writers have written extensively. "Scripture and Holy Tradition speak to us repeatedly about the Second Coming," writes Bishop Kallistos Ware.

They give us no grounds for supposing that, through a steady advance in "civilization", the world will grow gradually better and better until mankind succeeds in establishing God's kingdom on earth. The Christian view of world

[95] Augustine, *City of God*, XX, 9.

history is entirely opposed to this kind of evolutionary optimism. What we are taught to expect are disasters in the world of nature, increasingly destructive warfare between men, bewilderment and apostasy among those who call themselves Christians (see especially Matt. 24:3-27). The period of tribulation will culminate with the appearance of the 'man of sin' or Antichrist.[96]

Postmillennialism can easily be reconciled to the material and sensual desires of fallen man, for it suggests that by means of his wits, or even in spite of them, the world will step by step improve until it has become the kingdom of God. The utopian basis for such a doctrine is self evident, and Archbishop Averky spoke out passionately against it:

This false teaching wreaks terrible harm, lulling to sleep the spiritual vigilance of the faithful and suggesting to them that the end of the world is far away (if in fact there will be an end), and therefore there is no particular need to *watch and pray*, to which Christ the Saviour constantly called His followers (cf. Matt. 26:41), since everything in the world is gradually getting better and better, spiritual progress keeping step with materialism.[97]

---

[96] Bishop Kallistos Ware, *The Orthodox Way*, p. 134.
[97] Archbishop Averky Taushev, pp. 288-289.

Resurrection

The primary characteristic emphasized by St. John regarding those reigning with Christ during those thousand years is that they will have been resurrected. This resurrection refers to a sacrament of the Church, and is a mystery only comprehensible in the context of the Church, as Augustine says, "Therefore the Church even now is the kingdom of Christ, and the kingdom of heaven. Accordingly, even now His saints reign with Him, though otherwise than as they shall reign hereafter"[98] The nature and participants of this resurrection we shall examine in the next chapter.

[98] Augustine, *City of God,* XX, 8.

CHAPTER SEVEN

Resurrection from the Dead

Once a meeting of alcoholics brought in the renowned motivational speaker Julius Dahlberg to illustrate the dangers of drinking. Standing at the podium, Mr. Dahlberg displayed two glass containers full of clear liquid.

"In one of these containers," he declared to the gathered alcoholics, "is pure water. In the other is grain alcohol. Can any of you tell which is which?" Heads shook back and forth throughout the auditorium, as the containers appeared to be identical.

"But there is a simple way to determine which container holds healthy water and which one holds poison," Dahlberg announced. He held up two worms, which wriggled in his fingers. "First I am dropping a worm into this container," he said. "Let's see what happens." The worm plopped into the clear liquid and swam contentedly about."No problems there," the speaker said.

"But what happens when we put a worm into this container?" He dropped the second worm into the other container. The poor creature immediately began to writhe in agony. After a few seconds it grew limp and floated lifelessly to the bottom.

Mr. Dahlberg's face was aglow with anticipation as he scanned the gathered alcoholics. "What does this prove?" he asked breathlessly. Silence reigned over the auditorium. Finally a man in the back row stood up and said, "If you drink alcohol you'll never have worms."

When even the clearest messages on pragmatic subjects draw unexpected interpretations, no one should be surprised if the prophetic literature of the Holy Scriptures sometimes gives rise to multiple opinions about its ultimate meaning. Each person is inclined to read the text according to his own preconceptions and biases, and thereby read *into* the text meanings that the writer may never have intended.

This is why it is vital to reference the ancient patristic sources when studying the Scriptures. We should read as though God is speaking to us personally in that moment, yet also read humbly as members of the Church. We have no right to draw conclusions at odds from what believers who have gone before us understood to be true. And so it is with the theme of resurrection.

The dream of resurrecting from the dead has animated human imagination for eons. It is clear from the cycle of nature that all living things are mortal. Every sort of creature enjoys life on a temporary basis only. Indeed, death is, from our fallen point of view at least, part of life's natural sequence—its ultimate and unavoidable conclusion. Yet, man senses that he is, or ought to be, immortal. He cringes at the thought of absolute extinction. Physical death is humiliating and disrupting, but were it also to represent the end of personal identity, then existence would be meaningless.

Of course, this is precisely what nihilists claim. "*Nihil*" means "nothing," and nihilists believe there is nothing sentient in the universe—no ordering consciousness, no loving Presence above us all. On the level of individual experience their perception is logical. For if one has no relationship with Jesus Christ, Who is the resurrection and the life, then existence must ever seem devoid of depth and meaning. But nihilism is obviously an anti-philosophy that offers nothing coherent and useful to human understanding. It is the refuge of superficial thinkers who want to avoid personal responsibility.

On the other hand, a person who has penetrated the veil of intellectualization and entered the realm of intuitive understanding, however tentatively, comprehends that eternity is real and always present, as Mother Maria of Paris intimates,

> Anyone who has had this experience of eternity, if only once—such a person will find it hard to turn aside from this path: to him all comfort will seem ephemeral, all treasure valueless, all companions unnecessary, if amongst them he fails to see the One Companion, carrying his Cross.[99]

Among the Jews of apostolic times, controversy and discussion regarding the possibility of resurrection was

---

[99] Mother Maria of Paris: in Hackel, *One, of Great Price*, pp. 4-5.

common. The Sadducees quizzed Jesus on this issue by posing a convoluted story of a woman with seven husbands (Mat. 22:23-30). Nor was this a trivial issue among the Pharisees, as St. Paul demonstrated:

> But when Paul perceived that the one part were Sadducees, and the other Pharisees, he cried out in the council, Men and brethren, I am a Pharisee, the son of a Pharisee: of the hope and resurrection of the dead I am called in question. And when he had so said, there arose a dissension between the Pharisees and the Sadducees: and the multitude was divided. For the Sadducees say that there is no resurrection, neither angel, nor spirit: but the Pharisees confess both (Acts 23:6-8).

This resurrection in which the Pharisees believed was expected to happen sometime in the future when God restored the kingdom to Israel, which Martha reveals in speaking to the Lord: "Martha saith unto him, I know that he shall rise again in the resurrection at the last day" (John 11:24). The Jewish concept of resurrection was closely linked to their expectation of a future earthly kingdom of bliss in which God restores them to their homeland:

> Thus saith the Lord God; Behold, O my people, I will open your graves, and cause you to come up out of your graves, and bring you into the land of Israel. And ye shall know that I am the Lord, when I have opened your graves, O my people, and brought you up out of your graves.

And shall put my spirit in you, and ye shall live, and I shall place you in your own land (Ez. 37:12-14).

The Jewish Influence

As was pointed out earlier, the Jewish prophetic tradition of a future blessed time on earth strongly influenced some of the early Christian writers. The resurrection of the body into a near paradise provided an established paradigm that harmonized—from certain points-of-view, at least—with the greater clarity on these subjects given by Jesus and the Apostles.

Irenaeus appears to have taken his concept of resurrection almost exclusively from the Old Testament.

Isaiah has plainly declared that there shall be joy of this nature at the resurrection of the just when he says, "The dead shall rise again; those, too, who are in the tombs shall arise, and those who are in the earth shall rejoice. For the dew from Thee is health to them." And this again Ezekiel also says: "Behold, I will open your tombs, and will bring you forth out of your graves; when I will draw my people from the sepulchers, and I will put breath in you, and ye shall live; and I will place you in your own land, and ye shall know that I am the Lord"[100]

---

[100] Irenaeus, *Against Heresies*, Book 5:34:1.

Irenaeus insists that this resurrection is to come after Christ's return, and will be a material and physical experience. Taking his cue from the prophets, he conceives of a resurrection that will satisfy terms of the Old Covenant:

> Now all these things being such as they are, cannot be understood in reference to super-celestial matters; "for God," it is said, "will show to the whole earth that is under heaven thy glory." But in the times of the kingdom, the earth has been called again by Christ to its pristine condition), and Jerusalem rebuilt after the pattern of the Jerusalem above, of which the prophet Isaiah says, "Behold, I have depicted thy walls upon my hands, and thou art always in my sight."[101]

Yet, this premillennialist doctrine of life on earth for mankind after the second resurrection is categorically refuted by Rufinus, who writes, "The virtue of the resurrection confers on men an angelic state, so that they who have risen from the earth shall not live again on the earth with the brute animals but with angels in heaven."[102]

The Voice of the Sibyl

Lactantius was another early father whose view of the future resurrection of mankind was deeply influ-

[101] Irenaeus, *Against Heresies,* Book 5:35:2.
[102] Rufinus, *A Commentary on the Apostles' Creed,* 41.

enced by pre-Christian philosophy. He is not hesitant to admit that his vision relies heavily upon the Sibyls, whom he accords the respect of divine oracles:

> But let us return from human to divine things. The Sibyl thus speaks, "As many as are holy shall live again on the earth, God giving them at the same time a spirit, and honour, and life." Then they which shall be alive in their bodies shall not die, but during those thousand years shall produce an infinite multitude, and their offspring shall be holy, and beloved by God.[103]

The people Lactantius describes are those who, according to him, were dead and brought to life again at the Lord's second coming. Their resurrection comes at the commencement of a future blessed age that is to last for one thousand years. We have already learned what pleasures people are expected to enjoy then. "And then shall God give great joy to men; for the earth, and the trees, and the numberless flocks of the earth shall give to men the true fruit of the vine, and sweet honey, and white milk, and corn, which is the best of all things to mortals."[104]

Although people of that time will not die according to Lactantius, yet they shall not live the pure life of angels either. On the contrary, Lactantius indicates that copulation must perforce become a primary occupation, along with eating and drinking, since "they shall pro-

[103] Lactantius, *The Divine Institutes,* Book 7, XXIII-XXIV.
[104] Lactantius, *The Divine Institutes,* Book 7, XXIV.

duce an infinite multitude." Irenaeus takes up this theme also, saying, "And Jeremiah the prophet has pointed out, that as many believers as God has prepared for this purpose, to multiply those left on earth."[105] One might suppose that the task of those "prepared for this purpose" of multiplying would be highly coveted in the future blessed life.

Yet, one searches vainly in the New Testament for any scriptural confirmation of the scenario envisioned by Irenaeus and Lactantius. The Lord, in fact, sets quite another tone for that resurrection which is to occur at His second coming: It is the angelic life of the eternal kingdom. "For in the resurrection they neither marry, nor are given in marriage, but are as the angels of God in heaven" (Matt. 22:30).

Two Deaths

In disobeying God, our primal parents Adam and Eve died spiritually, in that their souls were separated from the Holy Spirit. This brought about the subsequent death of their bodies as well, as St. Symeon explains:

> Thus, in soul Adam died immediately, as soon as he had tasted; and later, after nine hundred and thirty years, he died also in body. For, as the death of the body is the separation from it of the soul, so the death of the soul is the separation from it of the Holy Spirit. Later, for this

[105] Irenaeus, *Against Heresies*, Book 5:35:1.

reason, the whole human race also became such as our forefather Adam became through the fall — mortal, that is, both in soul and body.[106]

Mortality, then, is the "first death," which all humans experience outwardly as the corruption and dying of their physical bodies, and inwardly as their isolation from God. Unless one is resurrected from this first death, he must endure the second death as well, and be "cast into the lake of fire. This is the second death. And whosoever was not found written in the book of life was cast into the lake of fire" (Rev. 20:14-15).

Thus, as the first death is separation of the soul from the Holy Spirit in time, the second death represents separation from the Holy Spirit in eternity. St. Andrew of Caesarea explains:

> From the Divine Scripture we know there are two lives and two deaths: the first life is temporal and fleshly because of the transgression of the commandments, while the second is the eternal life promised to the saints for the keeping of the Divine commandments. Corresponding to these there are two kinds of death: one fleshly and temporal, and the other eternal as a chastisement for sins, which is the fiery Gehenna.[107]

[106]St. Symeon the New Theologian, *The First Created Man*, p. 45.

[107] Archbishop Averky Taushev, p. 255.

The second death is the inevitable consequence of living for oneself on this earth, as the Lord indicated: "For whosoever will save his life shall lose it: and whosoever will lose his life for my sake shall save it" (Luke. 9:24). Unlike the first death, the second death is not for all, but only for those whose names are not written in the book of life. "The 'second death' is the judgment of sinners at the Last Judgment," says Michael Pomazansky:

> It will not touch those *who have part in the first resurrection* (Apoc. 20:6); this means that those who are spiritually reborn in Christ and purified by the grace of God in the Church will not be subjected to judgment, but will enter into the blessed life of the Kingdom of Christ.[108]

The second death represents the experience of eternity for those who are not in loving relationship with God. The enumeration of "fearful, unbelieving, abominable," etc., suggests the state of souls who love sin rather than God. "He that overcometh shall inherit all things; and I will be his God, and he shall be my son. But the fearful, and unbelieving, and the abominable, and murderers, and whoremongers, and sorcerers, and idolaters, and all liars, shall have their part in the lake which burneth with fire and brimstone: which is the second death" (Rev. 21:7-8).

---

[108] Fr. Michael Pomazansky, *Orthodox Dogmatic Theology* (Platina, CA: St. Herman of Alaska Brotherhood, 1984), p. 340.

Two Resurrections

Prior to the Christian era, there was ongoing debate among Jewish and Gentile philosophers about resurrection — not only whether it might really happen, but how and to what? If man could indeed rise from the dead, was it the body, or the soul alone, or both together that returned to life? Yet the Lord put all these questions to rest when He said, "I am the resurrection, and the life: he that believeth on me, though he were dead, yet shall he live" (John 11:25).

Jesus *is* the resurrection. This idea eludes the intellect and must be accepted on faith by the heart. Those who do this, who "believe on" Him, shall live. Jesus Christ, Who is the resurrection, has two comings on earth, one in humility and one in glory. His first coming, in lowliness, was unseen by most. His second coming, in majesty, shall be seen by all. The fathers indicate that, corresponding to these two comings of the Lord, there are two distinct resurrections of man.

St. John speaks of the first resurrection in Revelation:

> I saw thrones, and they sat upon them, and judgment was given unto them . . . and they lived and reigned with Christ a thousand years. But the rest of the dead lived not again until the thousand years were finished. This is the first resurrection. Blessed and holy is he who has part in the first resurrection: on such the second death shall have no power, but they shall be

priests of God and Christ, and they shall reign with Him a thousand years (Rev. 20:4-5).

Between the first and second resurrections, those who have been resurrected are said to live and reign with Christ for a figurative thousand years. This "living" and "reigning" does not refer to earthly activities, but rather the spiritual state of being in relationship with Christ through baptism into His Church. "Their 'living' is of a moral and spiritual nature," says Archbishop Averky.

> The holy Seer of Mysteries calls this "the first resurrection," while further on he speaks of the second bodily resurrection. This reigning of the saints with Christ will continue until the final victory over the dark impious powers under Antichrist. Then the resurrection of bodies will occur, and the last frightful judgment will begin, when the souls of the saints will be reunited with their bodies and live with Christ forever.[109]

The First Resurrection

The desire deep within man to return to the Garden of Eden, as it were, to be restored to his primal simplicity and unity of spirit, has been conceived in many cultures as a resurrection from the dead. There is a sense in which all people, though they may live and breathe, are dead. This is the death of sin, a characteris-

---

[109] Archbishop Averky Taushev, p. 254.

tic of our fallen human condition. Even one who lives a "good" life is in this sense dead, unless he is reborn in Christ. "For all have sinned, and come short of the glory of God," said St. Paul (Rom. 3:23).

Therefore, when the Lord said, "Repent, for the kingdom of heaven is at hand," (Matt. 4:17) He was addressing those dead in sin. So it is still, as the Gospel continues to be preached to each generation and soul. Some are able to hear Christ's voice, as He said: "Verily, verily I say unto you, the hour is coming, and now is, when the dead shall hear the voice of the Son of God: and they that hear shall live" (John 5:25).

The life that these receive is to enter into the kingdom of God. This is the first resurrection, of which St. Augustine speaks:

> Now this resurrection regards not the body, but the soul. For souls, too, have a death of their own in wickedness and sins. It is of these dead, then—the dead in ungodliness and wickedness—that He says, "The hour is coming and now is, when the dead shall hear the voice of the Son of God; and they that hear shall live." Here no difference is made between the good and the bad. For it is good for all men to hear His voice and live, by passing to the life of godliness from the life of ungodliness.[110]

Jesus came to earth that mankind might be able to receive the first resurrection. Man must still decide to

---

[110] Augustine, *City of God*, XX, 6.

accept it, but it is offered to all. The door is open, and the Master taps upon it, desiring that we would choose to enter into the life of faith. At this time and in this life, one can be resurrected — and be preserved from the second death. "The first resurrection is now of the souls that are by the faith," says Victorinus, "Which does not permit men to pass over into the second death."[111]

That the first resurrection is linked directly to faith in Christ is evident from Jesus' conversation with Martha:

> Jesus saith unto her, thy brother shall rise again. Martha saith unto him, I know that he shall rise again in the resurrection at the last day. Jesus saith unto her, I am the resurrection, and the life: he that believeth on me, though he were dead, yet shall he live: and whosoever liveth and believeth on me shall never die (John 11:23-25).

The devils also believe in God, but are not saved because their belief comes not of faith. We must believe here and now when heaven is hidden from our sight, like the blind man who does as those with eyes instruct him. "The hour is coming, and now is," says the Lord. Or, as St. Paul emphasizes, "Now is the accepted time; behold, now is the day of salvation" (2 Cor. 6:2). The time to hear Jesus is at hand; the only opportunity to repent and be saved is now. This first resurrection must

---

[111] Victorinus, *Commentary on the Apocalypse of the Blessed John*, XX, 5.

occur in one's natural lifetime, or it shall not occur at all.

The first resurrection was made possible when Christ bound the "strong man," at His first coming. And Satan is in a sense bound anew with each soul's deciding for the Lord, as Augustine says:

> Now the devil was thus bound not only when the Church began to be more and more widely extended among the nations beyond Judea, but is now and shall be bound till the end of the world, when he is to be loosed. Because even now men are, and doubtless to the end of the world shall be, converted to the faith from the unbelief in which he held them. And this strong one is bound in each instance in which he is spoiled of one of his goods.[112]

Therefore the first resurrection is the rejoining of soul with the Holy Spirit, which occurs at the rebirth of baptism, and which allows believers to say with St. Paul, "O death, where is thy sting? O grave, where is thy victory?" (1 Cor. 15:55). The sacrament of baptism is a symbol of burial, an acknowledgment that we were already dead spiritually. But in this dying is the seed of rebirth, as St. Paul says, "Buried with him in baptism, wherein also ye are risen with him through the faith of the operation of God, who hath raised him from the dead" (Col. 2:11).

---

[112] Augustine, *City of God*, XX, 8.

The Lord said that the dead would hear His voice, and that those who heard would live. It is the blind that seek sight, and the sick that seek healing. Those conscious of the life they do not have — of their spiritual deadness — turn to God like the lost souls of Hades. It is these who will be lifted up by Christ. "Even when we were dead in sins, [God] . . . hath raised us up together, and made us sit together in heavenly places in Christ Jesus" (Eph. 2:4-6).

Unlike the second resurrection, which is a requirement upon all, the first resurrection is totally voluntary. And for this reason the resulting judgment is severe upon those who reject it, since man by his own actions chooses whether to accept God's gift of life.

> This judgment He uses here in the same sense as a little before, when He says, "He that heareth my word, and believeth on Him that sent me, hath everlasting life, and shall not come into judgment, but is passed from death to life;" i.e., by having a part in the first resurrection, by which a transition from death to life is made in this present time, he shall not come into damnation, which He mentions by the name of judgment, as also in the place where he says, "but they that have done evil unto the resurrection of judgment," i.e., damnation. He, therefore, who would not be damned in the second resurrection, let him rise in the first."[113]

---

[113] Augustine, *City of God,* XX, 6.

St. John Chrysostom's Sermon of Resurrection

This first resurrection of believers is brought about by Christ's resurrection from the dead and experienced through baptism within the Church. These things are conveyed in the incomparable Easter Sermon of St. John Chrysostom (who was born in Antioch in the year 347), which is read in every Orthodox Church during the Paschal Liturgy:

Let no one fear death, for the Savior's death has set us free. He who was held prisoner of it, has annihilated it. By descending into Hell, he has made Hell captive. He angered it when it tasted of his flesh. And Isaiah, foretelling this, did cry: Hell, said he, was angered, when it encountered You in the lower regions. It was angered for it was abolished. It was angered, for it was mocked. It was angered, for it was slain. It was angered for it was overthrown. It was angered, for it was fettered in chains. It took a body, and met God face to face. It took earth, and encountered Heaven. It took that which was seen, and fell upon the unseen. O Death, where is your sting? O Hell, where is your victory? Christ is risen, and you are overthrown. Christ is risen, and the demons are fallen. Christ is risen, and the Angels rejoice. Christ is risen, and life reigns. Christ is risen, and not one dead remains in the grave. For Christ, being risen from the dead, has become the first-fruits of those who have fallen asleep. To Him be glory and dominion unto ages of ages. Amen."[114]

Those Who Did Not Live

But what is meant by St. John's statement, "the rest of the dead lived not again until the thousand years were finished"? Our Lord says those that hear His voice shall live. Therefore those who do not hear (though the words of Life are also spoken to them) shall not live. They shall not be resurrected in the first resurrection, and shall not enter the kingdom of God. They shall not reign with Christ for a thousand years.

Archbishop Averky writes,

> The expression "lived not again" means the dark and difficult condition of the souls of the impious sinners after bodily death. It continues "until the thousand years were finished." As in many other places in Sacred Scripture, this particle "until" (in Greek *eos*) does not signify the continuation of an action only to a certain boundary; on the contrary, it is a complete denial of any limit. In other words, it means the impious dead are denied *forever* the blessed life.[115]

---

[114] Quoted in *The Bible and the Holy Fathers for Orthodox* (Menlo Park, CA: Monastery Books), 1990, p. 11.

[115] Archbishop Averky Taushev, p. 255.

All humans were at one time dead. Those that hear the voice of the Lord are restored again to life in the first resurrection, and brought into the eternal kingdom in the second resurrection. But those dead who do not hear the voice of the Lord can never live again. In this earthly life when they could have been baptized and entered the Church, they did not. As St. Augustine says,

They did not live in the time in which they ought to have lived by passing from death to life. And therefore, when the day of the bodily resurrection arrives, they shall come out of their graves, not to life, but to judgment, namely, to damnation, which is called the second death. For whosoever has not lived until the thousand years be finished, i.e., during this whole time in which the first resurrection is going on — whosoever has not heard the voice of the Son of God, and passed from death to life,--that man shall certainly in the second resurrection, the resurrection of the flesh, pass with his flesh into the second death.[116]

The Second Resurrection

And yet there is a second resurrection in which all people will participate without exception, whether they will or no. Our Lord describes it thus: "Marvel not at this: for the hour is coming, in the which all that are in

---

[116] Augustine, *City of God*, XX, 9.

the graves shall hear his voice, and shall come forth; they that have done good, unto the resurrection of life; and they that have done evil, unto the resurrection of damnation" (John 5:28-29).

Here, the Lord does not say, "the hour is coming and now is," for this resurrection takes place not in this life, but rather at the end of the age when Christ shall judge the world. Here He speaks not of the "dead," that is, the non-baptized, but rather all in the graves, indicating all souls who have existed upon the earth. Nor does He say, as in the first resurrection, "and they that hear shall live." For all shall, indeed, hear His voice this time, but not all shall live.

It is this second resurrection, that which will occur at our Lord's second coming and His judgment, of which St. Paul speaks when he says, "Who concerning the truth have erred, saying that the resurrection is past already; and overthrown the faith of some" (2 Tim. 2:18). It is this second resurrection to which the martyrs have looked when they "were tortured, not accepting deliverance; that they might obtain a better resurrection" (Heb. 11:35).

As there are two comings of Christ, Who is the Resurrection, so are there two resurrections for man. Where there is a resurrection, there must first be a death, so there are likewise two deaths. These have different characteristics, but are intimately related. He that experiences the first resurrection is spared the second death.

There are two resurrections. The one the first and spiritual resurrection, which has place in this life, and preserves us from coming into the second death; and the other the second, which does not occur now, but in the end of the world, and which is of the body, not of the soul, and which by the last judgment shall dismiss some into the second death, others into that life which has no death.[117]

The Lord encourages Christians to be "faithful unto death." We are not to fear the death of the body, as that is inevitable in any case. "Fortunate is he who endures all these temporal chastisements with gratitude, confessing that he has been justly condemned to them for the ancestral sin," writes St. Symeon.

Yea, he will find repose for his labors; for by reason of these chastisements the All-good God has given death to men, so that those who bear them with gratitude might rest from them for a time, and then might be resurrected and glorified in the day of judgment through the new Adam, the sinless Jesus Christ.[118]

We are to bear sufferings, even *tribulation*. It is only possible to be faithful unto death when one has already a connection with eternity in the first resurrection. "Fear none of those things which thou shalt suffer," said the Lord. "Behold, the devil shall cast some of you into prison, that ye may be tried; and ye shall have tribulation ten days: be thou faithful unto death, and I

---

[117] Augustine, *City of God*, XX, 6.
[118] Symeon the New Theologian, *The First Created Man*, p. 61.

will give thee a crown of life.... He that overcometh shall not be hurt of the second death" (Rev. 2:10-11).

The prophetic traditions are developed and clarified in the words of Christ and His Apostles. From these we learn that the resurrection will indeed be of the whole man, body and soul, but that the life to which he comes is not one of earthly and material delights.

> From the word of God one must conclude that the resurrected bodies will be *essentially* the same ones that belonged to their souls in this earthly life: *THIS corruptible must put on incorruption, and THIS mortal must put on immortality* (1 Cor. 15:53). But at the same time, they will be transfigured, and first of all, the bodies of the righteous will be incorrupt and immortal, as is evident from the same words of the Apostle.[119]

Life can never become non-life; being can never become non-being. Therefore all souls who have lived shall live forever. The only question is, how shall they experience eternity — in bliss or misery? Not only are godly souls to be resurrected, but ungodly ones as well.

The Two Doors

The two resurrections just described are portrayed in Scripture as the doors to eternal life. Salvation means only one thing, which is to live eternally in God's loving

---

[119] Fr. Michael Pomazansky, *Orthodox Dogmatic Theology*, p. 340.

presence. The Lord taught that salvation is available to all, but that many will not choose it.

> Then one said unto him, Lord, are there few that be saved? And he said unto them, strive to enter in at the strait gate: for many, I say unto you, will seek to enter in, and shall not be able. When once the master of the house is risen up, and hath shut to the door, and ye begin to stand without, and to knock at the door, saying, Lord, Lord, open unto us; and he shall answer and say unto you, I know you not whence you are: Then shall ye begin to say, we have eaten and drunk in thy presence, and thou hast taught in our streets. But he shall say, I tell you, I know you not (Luke 13:23-27).

Here Jesus tells us to "strive to enter." This is a present-tense verb—it is something we can do now, if only we will. The strait gate through which we must go does not reject any willing supplicant. It is strait not because it refuses admittance to those would enter, but because it is the only gate to the kingdom, and all must gain access by it alone. The only way to heaven is Jesus Himself—He is the gate, as He said, "I am the door: by me if any man enter in, he shall be saved" (John 10:9).

After telling His followers to enter the strait gate, Jesus says, "for many... will seek to enter in, and shall not be able." They *will* seek—in the times of the second resurrection. They will then see plainly what before could only be apprehended through faith. Their spiritual eyes will be opened and they will understand for the first time that during their earthly lives they had actually (though unknowingly) eaten and drunk in the Master's presence and that He had taught in their streets.

But whosoever has not passed through the first door shall not enter the second. For once the time of voluntary action is past, when the opportunity for repentance has ended, then the master of the house will close the door. Then those who sought their own way instead of God's will realize their foolishness and desire to be part of the eternal kingdom — but too late.

Another parable speaks of a door being the passage to the Lord's presence — a door that remains shut against those who did not prepare themselves for His coming. In this case, the preparation is characterized as wise virgins having oil for their lamps when the Bridegroom comes, which Orthodox will recognize as the chrism of baptism and the seal of the gift of the Holy Spirit (Mat. 25:1-13).

How is it possible that our God, Who is omniscient, will say, "I know you not"? For in both of these parables these are the words spoken to those unfortunates who are unprepared for His coming. Jesus clarifies this in describing the good shepherd Who is in relationship with his flock — they know Him, and He knows them: "I am the good shepherd, and know my sheep, and am know of mine" (John 10:14). Those who do not commune with the Lord through faith will not be known to Him when He appears before the world in His glory.

It might be said that there is one door and one right time for entering that door. The time is now, before the

Lord's Second Coming. Jesus encourages all to enter now: "Behold, I stand at the door and knock: if any man hear my voice, and open the door, I will come in to him, and will sup with him, and he with me" (Rev. 3:20). Here is represented the first resurrection, in which those who have entered reign with Christ. They eat and drink in His presence, the Holy Spirit being operative in their lives. And here also is that feast which premillennialists have misunderstood—it is communion with Christ, Whose "flesh is meat indeed," and Whose "blood is drink indeed" (John 6:55).

Yet the time of repentance is not forever. Those who waste their precious opportunity and remain supine when faith no bigger than a mustard seed would have secured their entrance will suddenly wake to find the Lord is present. Then faith will no longer be an issue, for He will be undeniably visible to all. At that time many will suddenly desire to enter the kingdom of God. They will perceive the error of their ways and want to make amends. And the door which formerly had needed but the push of weakened mankind's repentant hand in order to open will have closed from God's side. Those without will desperately pound in vain where formerly the Lord had meekly tapped.

Spiritualized?

It is vogue among modern premillennialists to accuse this traditional Orthodox teaching about the resurrection of having been "spiritualized." They suggest it does not follow from a literal interpretation of the Bible (which interpretation, they assert, would yield a premillennial understanding of the two resurrections, placing them both far in the future after the Lord's second coming).

The concise answer to such a claim is that it flies in the face of twenty centuries of unambiguous Christian doctrine. The interpretation has lasted over time because it is in accord with a coherent body of Christian thought preserved since apostolic and patristic times. More importantly (and this point is never mentioned by premillennialists) its truth has been borne out in the lives of authentic Christians over those two millennia. Saints exist because there is a real kingdom of heaven into which they enter *in this life!* These are not effluvious theories, but rather firm realities that have been and continue to be experienced by those who have entered the strait gate of baptism into the Holy Spirit.

Michael Pomazansky's analysis of the premillennialist philosophy hits the nail on the head:

> Formally, this teaching is based on an incorrect understanding of the expression 'the first resurrection'; while inwardly, its cause is rooted in the loss, among the masses of contemporary sectarianism, of faith in life after death, in the blessedness of the righteous in heaven (with whom they have no communion in prayer); and another cause, in certain sects, is to be found in the utopian dreams for society hidden behind

religious ideas and inserted into the mysterious images of the Apocalypse.[120]

Materialized!

A far more compelling and accurate argument can be made that premillennialists inappropriately *materialize* the meaning of Biblical texts. And a literal interpretation of the Scriptures can provide no real guidance when the underlying presuppositions are completely wrong.

To illustrate this we need look no further than Tim LaHaye, author of the popular "Left Behind" series of books. LaHaye, who presents his case for dispensational premillennialism in *Revelation Unveiled*, writes,

> Somewhere, high in the heavens, out in the universe, a throne is set, which is the throne of God . . . Although the heavens are filled with stars wherever the telescope can reach, it seems that behind the North Star there is an empty space. For that reason it has been suggested that this could be the third heaven, the heaven of God, where His throne is.[121]

These words seem like the opening lines of a fairy tale. Are we to suppose that God's heaven is somewhere in the physical universe and locatable by

[120] Fr. Michael Pomazansky, *Orthodox Dogmatic Theology*, p. 342-343.
[121] Tim LaHaye, *Revelation Unveiled*, (Grand Rapids, MI: Zondervan Publishing House, 1999), p. 113.

Cartesian coordinates? If so, then astronomers should be able to calculate how many light years away it is. And astronauts might plan to get there not through prayer but with powerful rockets. Perhaps the Hubble telescope can clandestinely pry into God's marvelous activities!

Another example of materializing Scriptural themes can be noted in Hal Lindsey's description of heaven. His cartoon-like depiction is not qualitatively different than LaHaye's: "As a believer," says Lindsey, "I'm not especially interested in sitting on a cloud and plucking a harp night and day!"[122]

Such earthly concepts of spiritual realities call to mind the foolish Babylonians who thought to build a tower high enough to reach God. Although the word "heaven" is often utilized in reference to the physical sky, it also has an altogether spiritual meaning, that of the Almighty Himself. "The kingdom of heaven is within you," said Christ. This does not mean that air, sun moon, stars, etc., are inside us, but rather that God, being divine Spirit, is found and known by means of man's inner spirit.

[122] Hal Lindsey, *There's a New World Coming* (New York: Bantam Books, 1973), p. 113.

CHAPTER EIGHT

The Strong Man Unchained

John Tertle once came to visit an old acquaintance in New York. John had never been to the Big Apple before, so his friend Henry took him to eat at a popular café. They were immersed in conversation when from somewhere in the room a voice called out, "Twelve!"

At once, the café patrons erupted in laughter. Even the servers stopped what they were doing and guffawed. John gazed about, but could see no reason for their mirth. A few minutes later someone else yelled, "Twenty-four!" As before, the entire room was immediately engulfed in hilarity. Even Henry chuckled merrily. At this John's curiosity was piqued. "What on earth is so funny?" he asked his friend.

"Well you see, we've been telling amusing stories here for so long that we all know them by heart," explained Henry. "So now when someone calls out a story's number, we remember the whole thing down to the punch line. That's why everyone's laughing."

"That's fantastic!" said John. "Say, do you think I could try it?"

"Of course," Henry agreed.

John grinned, then cupped his hands around his mouth. "Seven!" he shouted. But instead of uproarious laughter, dead silence greeted his ears. The patrons continued to eat and converse among themselves as though they had heard nothing.

John took a deep breath. "Fifteen!" he bellowed at the top of his lungs. Again, there was no discernable response from the other people present. No rolling in the isles, no clutching at the sides, no gasping for breath. John looked to Henry for explanation. "What's wrong?" He asked. "Why aren't they laughing?"

"Well," Henry replied, obviously embarrassed for his friend. "Some people just can't tell a joke."

We might draw a parallel between this story and understanding the Holy Scriptures. The Bible is a set of words—divinely inspired, of course, but words nonetheless—which describe and refer to spiritual realities. There is a particular way of understanding these words, an interpretation passed down intact from the fathers, with which our souls can resonate. We hear and agree, we comprehend, we grasp the significance, or as the above story would have it, we "get it" and respond affirmatively.

On the other hand, there are other interpretations somehow out of kilter with the tradition. We may hear them, but they do not produce the appropriate response. They confuse rather than clarify. Instead of eliciting a common understanding, they generate division and opinion. Such interpretations are often called heresies.

The millennium is just such a subject. It has given rise, especially in modern times, to a variety of opinions not in harmony or concordance with the common and coherent understanding of the Church. Such opinions, even when broadcast around the earth, do not resonate in our souls. Unfortunately, they do affect the superficial thinking of many people, which is why this book was written.

In the Book of Revelation St. John speaks of a thousand years during which Satan is to be bound (Rev. 20:1-3). In this passage we see that Satan's incarceration has a definite conclusion at the end of a thousand years, when "he must be loosed a little season." Concurrent with this period of the Devil's bondage is the millennium of Christ's Church on earth: "And I saw thrones, and them that sat upon them, and judgment was given unto them . . . and they reigned with Christ for a thousand years" (Rev. 20:4). Here, however, there is no indication of the saints' reign ending, even when the thousand years are fulfilled. We are not told that they step down from their thrones or stop judging at the end of a thousand years, only that their reign lasts throughout that span.

There is general accord among patristic and modern writers that these two thousand-year periods — that of Satan's bondage and the Church's reign — are concurrent in time. As has been pointed out already however, there is a fundamental difference between the Orthodox and the premillennial point of view as to when this millennium is to begin.

Premillennialism holds that the thousand-year period of Christ's reign of grace on earth and Satan's simultaneous bondage are yet to occur. According to premillennialism, these things will not happen until after the Great Tribulation and will be inaugurated by the Lord's Second Advent. And then, after the thousand years (whether actual or metaphorical) are completed, the devil is to be released again for a short time.

Orthodoxy, on the other hand, teaches that this millennium of grace is happening now, and will be concluded at the Lord's return. We have already examined the first and second resurrection, now let us consider other Scriptural indicators which will shed light on the question of premillennialism. For instance, what of the "little season" of the devil's loosing? From the premillennial perspective there is no explanation for this loosing at the end of a thousand years of earthly delights. Neither in Scripture nor in reason itself can any sense be made of it. The premillennial scenario in fact forces out of alignment certain things that should be considered as varied descriptions of the same event.

By contrast, the Orthodox Christian teaching (sometimes inaccurately labeled "amillennialism") clarifies these relationships and puts them in proper perspective. In the first place, Christ's thousand-year reign on earth and Satan's concurrent bondage are not viewed as future events, but rather as ones taking place even now. The thousand-year period began at the Lord's first advent, and will conclude at His second. This allows us to view human history in a new light, as in fact having a sacred dimension, in that it has a part to play in leading to the end of the world.

From the Orthodox point of view we can easily understand that the loosing of Satan for a little season corresponds with the three and a half years of Great

Tribulation and the short reign of Antichrist. Patristic writers make a clear connection between Satan's being loosed anew upon the world (after a thousand years of bondage) and his operating through Antichrist, as Archbishop Averky points out: "By the 'loosing of Satan out of his prison' is to be understood the appearance of Antichrist before the end of the world. The liberated Satan will strive in the person of Antichrist to deceive all the nations of the earth."[123]

We can further understand that the spread into the world of the Christian Church has occurred because Satan was bound. But what is the meaning of his being unbound? Is there a specific correlation between this and the appearance of Antichrist, and are there other Scriptural indicators of when these things are to happen?

The Nature of Antichrist

Although science fiction writers have portrayed many horrible creatures — vampires, werewolves, men sewed together and restored to life by lightning bolts and so forth — none of these even approximates the accumulated horror that is supposed to be manifested in Antichrist. Who is this being, of which the Lord Himself gave warning?

Irenaeus says that Antichrist will not merely be evil, but will recapitulate in himself all evils in human and angelic history:

---

[123] Archbishop Averky Taushev, p. 258.

And there is therefore in this beast, when he comes, a recapitulation made of all sorts of iniquity and of every deceit, in order that all apostate power, flowing into and being shut up in him, may be sent into the furnace of fire. Fittingly, therefore, shall his name possess the number six hundred and sixty-six, since he sums up in his own person all the commixture of wickedness which took place previous to the deluge, due to the apostasy of the angels. For Noah was six hundred years old when the deluge came upon the earth, sweeping away the rebellious world, for the sake of that most infamous generation which lived in the times of Noah. And [Antichrist] also sums up every error of devised idols since the flood, together with the slaying of the prophets and the cutting off of the just.[124]

Some have thought Antichrist will not be human, but rather a spirit. The fathers clearly state however, that he will be a man whose will is completely given over to evil. As Jesus perfectly executed the will of His Father in heaven, so Antichrist will perfectly carry out the will of Satan. "Satan has used him as an instrument," says St. Cyril of Jerusalem, "working in his own person through him."[125] Archbishop Averky says, "Antichrist will not be some kind of spirit or demon, but a

---

[124] Irenaeus, *Against Heresies*, 5:29:2.
[125] Cyril of Jerusalem, *Catechetical Lectures*, XV, 14.

heinous offspring of the human race. He will not be an incarnate devil, as some have thought, but a man."[126]

He will endeavor to be accepted through appearing not evil, but good—even divine. He will go so far as to imitate our Lord Jesus Christ Himself, as Hippolytus points out:

> For in every respect that deceiver seeks to make himself appear like the Son of God. Christ is a lion, and Antichrist is a lion. Christ is King of things celestial and things terrestrial, and Antichrist will be king upon earth. The Saviour was manifested as a lamb; and he, too, will appear as a lamb, while he is a wolf within... Christ arose from among the Hebrews, and he will spring from among the Jews. Christ displayed His flesh like a temple, and raised it up on the third day; and he too will raise up again the temple of stone in Jerusalem.[127]

According to the prophecies, Antichrist will exert more human authority than any person in history. He will be the first and last man capable of overpowering the whole world. Perhaps Jesus was thinking of Antichrist when He said, "What is a man advantaged, if he gain the whole world, and lose himself, or be cast away?" (Luke 9:25).

The Scriptures indeed speak of the beast being cast into the lake of fire after his defeat by Jesus. But before

---

[126]Archbishop Averky Taushev, p. 187.

[127] Hippolytus, *Appendix to the Works of Hippolytus,* XX.

that, he is destined to be received enthusiastically by those who rejected their Messiah, as the Lord warned: "I am come in my Father's name, and ye receive me not: if another shall come in his own name, him ye will receive" (John 5:43).

Antichrist will come in no other name but his own, claiming all authority and privilege, while making his arrogation appear not only correct but also beneficial to those who are surrendering their freedom.

> For he [Antichrist] will call together all the people to himself, out of every country of the dispersion, making them his own, as though they were his own children, and promising to restore their country, and establish again their kingdom and nation, in order that he may be worshipped by them as God.... For he will allure mankind to himself, wishing to gain possession of those who are not his own, and promising deliverance to all, while he is unable to save himself.[128]

Waiting On the Devil

Yet, Antichrist is not to appear until the world has been made ready for him. Satan must first be loosed and unbridled after his thousand years of bondage, in order to bring the masses of humanity to a degrading degree of receptivity of evil in which they will not only

[128] Hippolytus, *Works of Hippolytus,* II, 54.

accept, but also even welcome his protégé. This is the "falling away" described by St. Paul:

> Let no man deceive you by any means: for that day shall not come, except there come a falling away first, and that the man of sin be revealed, the son of perdition; Who opposeth and exalteth himself above all that is called God, or that is worshiped; so that he as God sitteth in the temple of God, showing himself that he is God. Remember ye not, that when I was yet with you, I told you these things?   And now ye know what withholdeth that he might be revealed in his time (2 Thes. 2:3-5).

"That day," is the day of the Lord, or Christ's Second Advent. This will not come, St. Paul says, until a falling away occurs, that is, until the world looses its Christian sense. When this occurs, the man of sin will be revealed. "And then shall the wicked be revealed," repeats St. Augustine. "No one doubts that this means Antichrist."[129] Though a man, he is clearly identified with Satan, for his "coming is after the working of Satan."

The Withholding One

St. Paul says the Wicked will be revealed "in his time." There is a time appointed for the world's exposure to this great evil. Until then, Satan is restricted—allowed no longer to work openly but only as "the mys-

---

[129] Augustine, *City of God*, XX, 19.

owed no longer to work openly but only as "the mystery of iniquity."

> For the mystery of iniquity doth already work: only he who now holds will hold, until he be taken out of the way. And then shall that Wicked be revealed, whom the Lord shall consume with the spirit of his mouth, and shall destroy with the brightness of his coming: Even him, whose coming is after the working of Satan with all power and lying wonders (2 Thes. 2:6-9).

Only after Satan is finally loosed will Antichrist be permitted to appear before men. In the meantime somebody or something "withholds" Satan until at the end of the last days "he be taken out of the way," allowing the evil one to escape his chains.

We can only envy the Thessalonians for their private conversations with St. Paul. "Don't you remember that I told you these things?" he asks. Though St. Augustine frankly admits that he does not know exactly "what withholds," he is willing to assume, as many others also have, that this represents Roman authority. "Some think that the Apostle Paul referred to the Roman Empire," he wrote, "and that he was unwilling to use language more explicit, lest he should incur the calumnious charge of wishing ill to the empire which it was hoped would be eternal. It is not absurd to believe that these words of the apostle refer to the Roman Empire."[130]

The Kingdom Given Away

How is it that Rome, which had dominion over much of the world, including the Jews, could be the withholding one? Jesus Christ came to the Jews, for He even laments, "O Jerusalem, Jerusalem, which killest the prophets and stonest them that are sent unto thee; how often would I have gathered thy children together, as a hen doth gather her brood under her wings, and ye would not" (Luke 13:34). The Jews would not, therefore the bounty of the Lord was given to others, as He warned: "The kingdom of God shall be taken from you and given to a nation bringing forth the fruits thereof" (Mat. 21:43).

This new nation was already at hand, for Judea was part of the Roman Empire. The first miracle recorded in Luke after the calling of Christ's disciples benefited not a Jew, but a Gentile. A Roman centurion asked Jesus to heal his servant by merely speaking a word, for he understood authority. Here the scriptures tell us of one of only two times that Jesus is said to have "marveled." The first is at the faithlessness of the Jews: "he marveled because of their unbelief" (Mk 6:6). The second is this instance, in which after the centurion explained that Jesus did not need to come in person to heal his servant the Lord, "marveled, and said to them that followed,

---

[130] Augustine, *City of God*, XX, 19.

Verily I say unto you, I have not found so great faith, no, not in Israel" (Mat. 8:10). Two things amazed the Lord: the hard-heartedness of those He came to save, and the faith of those who were not of Israel.

This centurion in a sense may represent the spiritual openness and fertility of the Roman Empire, which so craved the Light of Truth that (in spite of the opposition of some early Caesars) this formerly pagan civilization was fully Christianized within three hundred years. And lest this seem a long period of time, remember that such a renewal and regeneration has *yet* to be accomplished—two thousand years later—among the Jews!

Therefore, Roman authority was transformed from persecutor to protector of Christianity. St. Paul undoubtedly foresaw what was to become even more evident in the centuries to follow: "When Roman authority ceases," wrote St. John Chrysostom, "then he [Antichrist] will come. And rightfully so, because as long as people will be afraid of this government, no one will hasten to submit himself to Antichrist; but after it has been destroyed, anarchy will abide, and he will strive to steal all, both human and divine authority."

The Holy Spirit?

Writers outside the Orthodox tradition typically assert that the withholding one to which St. Paul referred must be the Holy Spirit. Tim LaHaye claims, "The restrainer in 2 Thessalonians 2:7, and the only restraining influence in society today, is the Holy Spirit within the church. When the church is raptured at the beginning of the Tribulation, the Holy Spirit, who dwells in the church, will be gone."[131]

Grant Jeffrey sides with him, saying, "Unless the Holy Spirit is taken out of the way in His office as Counselor, Antichrist will not be able to be revealed."[132] (Like scores of other chagrined premillennialists, Jeffrey also mistakenly thought he could figure out the date of Christ's return and wrote, "the year A.D. 2000 is a probable termination point for the 'last days."[133])

But on what Scriptural basis do these Protestant writers, for whom the Bible is supposedly sole authority, make such a bold claim? Jeffrey says, "John 16:8-11 makes it clear that the Holy Spirit is He that restrains the Antichrist."[134] Consider the passage he cites: "And when he is come, he will reprove the world of sin, and of righteousness, and of judgment: of sin, because they believe not on me; of righteousness, because I go to my Father, and ye see me no more; of judgment, because the prince of this world is judged." What in these words specifically states — or even vaguely suggests — that the Holy Spirit is the withholding one of which St. Paul spoke?

Beyond lacking Biblical verification for their point, no little presumption is shown, for what man can declare where the Holy Spirit may or may not be? The

[131] Tim LaHaye, *Rapture,* p. 113.
[132] Grant R. Jeffrey, *Armageddon: Appointment with Destiny* (New York: Bantam Books, 1990), p. 138.
[133] Jeffrey, p. 193.
[134] Jeffrey, p. 138

Lord Himself says, "The wind bloweth where it willeth, and thou hearest the sound of it, but canst not tell from where it cometh, and where it goeth; so is everyone that is born of the Spirit" (John 3:8). In other words, the Holy Spirit, being the third Person of the Holy Trinity, is well beyond human ken. We may (or may not!) perceive when it is guiding us, but we can make no claims regarding its movements and whereabouts. Furthermore, how can God's Holy Spirit, Who is "everywhere present and fillest all things," ever be removed from any created object at all?

Roman Authority

If, on the other hand, we conceive the withholding one to represent "Roman authority," then a clearer picture suddenly emerges. Unlike the Holy Spirit, the presence or absence of Roman authority is relatively easy to ascertain. Especially if we consider that what St. John Chrysostom surely meant by this authority was not so much the political and administrative heritage of the Roman Empire, but rather the spiritual, as manifested in the Orthodox Christian monarchy.

This legacy, which began in the fourth century with Constantine the Great, moved with the emperor to Byzantium. According to the verdict of the First Ecumenical Council, held in Constantinople in 381 A.D., "Constantinople is the New Rome" (or second Rome). Constantinople continued to be the seat of the Roman Christian monarchy until its fall to the Ottoman Turks in the year 1453.

After the loss of Constantinople, a tradition emerged according to which the Christian monarchy had passed from Byzantine to Russian emperors. "The most arresting tenet of the Orthodox theologians was the doctrine of the 'Third Rome,'" writes Robert Wallace. "It held that the first Rome had fallen into heresy, and as a punishment had been overthrown by barbarians. The second Rome, Byzantium, had also become heretical—in acknowledging the supremacy of the pope, at the Council of Florence in 1438—and consequently had been overrun by the Turks. The third Rome was Moscow, the capital of the last truly Christian nation on earth, and the residence of a czar who in his power was 'similar to God in heaven.'"[135]

Given our knowledge of subsequent world history, it is possible to accept both the third Rome doctrine and the prophetic insight of Monk Filofei, who wrote to the reigning czar centuries ago that, "all [Orthodox] Christian kingdoms have merged into your tsardom. Henceforth we can expect only one kingdom to come. That kingdom is eternal. Two Romes have fallen. The third stands firm. And there will not be a fourth. No one will replace your Christian tsardom."

The Loss of Christian Authority

Lactantius had stated that Antichrist's reign of terror could only become possible after Roman Christian

---

[135] Robert Wallace, *Rise of Russia* (New York: Time-Life Books, 1967), p. 64.

authority was removed from the world: "The cause of this desolation and confusion will be this; because the Roman name, by which the earth is now ruled, will be taken away from the earth."[136]

A patristic writer from the 1800's, Saint Theophan the Recluse, anticipated the worldwide evil which would attend the loss of Christian authority: "When the monarchy falls," he said, "and everywhere nations institute self-government (republics, democracies), then the Antichrist will be able to act freely. It will not be difficult for Satan to prepare voters to renounce Christ, as experience taught us during the French Revolution. There will be no one to veto the movement... Thus, when such a social order is instituted everywhere, making it easy for antichristian movements to appear, then the Antichrist will come forth."[137]

If Moscow was indeed the third "Rome" and if the Russian Czars were indeed the inheritors of that Roman monarchical authority, then it is possible to name the precise date on which the fall described by St. Theophan occurred. The Roman name was "taken away from the world" on July 17, 1918, when atheist Bolshevik Communists assassinated Tsar Nicholas II.

Tsar Nicholas II, a member of the aptly named *Romanov* dynasty, was the last anointed monarch in the line of Constantine the Great, and his untimely death broke a succession that had lasted some fifteen hundred years. Because of this, the tsar's murder transcends per-

[136] Lactantius, *The Divine Institutes*, Book VII, 15.
[137] Theophan the Recluse, *A Ray of Light*.

sonal or national issues and represents an event of worldwide significance in sacred history.

Father Gleb Yakunin, who personally suffered at the hands of Communist torturers, said, "The meaning for world history of the martyr's death of the Imperial Family, something that likens it to the most significant Biblical events, consists of the fact that here the Constantinopolitan period of the existence of the Church of Christ comes to an end, and a new, martyric, apocalyptic age opens up. It is begun with the voluntary sacrifice of the last anointed Orthodox Emperor and his family."[138]

To the writings of Church fathers, other modern testimonies can be added. Archimandrite Constantine of Jordanville wrote, "The fall of Russia signaled a beginning to the pre-Antichrist epoch through which we are currently living. This cataclysm did away with the 'restraining power' in the world, setting Satan free from his temporary (thousand year, as the Scriptures allegorically call it) bondage."[139]

Since that fateful moment in 1918 the world has entered an unprecedented period of anarchy and disorder. Two world wars and an unending series of lesser conflicts have claimed millions of lives. Epidemics, AIDS, atomic warfare, Communism, Fascism, and a myriad of other evils have been woven into the history of these times. Satan works unbridled to prepare the

[138] Quoted by Fr. Seraphim Rose, *Heavenly Realm*, p. 94.
[139] Archimandrite Constantine, *Ecumenism, Communism and Apostasy*, p.3.

way for his protégé, Antichrist. No longer restricted as the mystery of iniquity, Satan hastens to bring about the "falling away" of which St. Paul warned. Priest Paul Volmensky called "the murder of Czar Nicholas II . . . a precise indicator that Antichrist is at the door and behind him is the Second Coming of Christ and the Last Judgment. The 'withholder' has been *taken out of the way* and Satan works unbridled."[140]

Sympathy For The Devil

Some Christians, even within Orthodoxy, question the foregoing view of the tsar's role in sacred history. Therefore this author wishes to thank alert reader James Jenkins for bringing to his attention a rather remarkable "document" that offers, in its own unique way, a similar yet surely unbiased view of the last Christian monarch in the line of Constantine. Although this document is non-patristic, the light it sheds on the question at hand is most interesting.

In 1968, the Rolling Stones released a record album called Beggars Banquet. The lead song on this album, "Sympathy for the Devil," quickly developed a reputation of bringing out the worst in people. Singer Mick Jagger is reported to have said that something bad always happened whenever the band played that song, and at least one person was stabbed to death at a con-

---

[140] Fr. Paul Volmensky, "In Memory of the 75th Anniversary of the Murder of Czar Martyr Nicholas II, *Orthodox Life*, 43:4 (July-August 1993), p. 2.

cert when it was performed. The partial lyrics are as follows:

SYMPATHY FOR THE DEVIL

Please allow me to introduce myself
I'm a man of wealth and taste
I've been around for a long, long year
Stole many a man's soul and faith

I was 'round when Jesus Christ
Had His moment of doubt and pain
Made damn sure that Pilate
Washed his hands and sealed his fate

(Refrain):
Pleased to meet you
Hope you guess my name
But what's puzzling you
Is the nature of my game

I stuck around St. Petersburg
When I saw it was time for a change
Killed the czar and his ministers
Anastasia screamed in vain

I rode a tank
Held a general's rank
When the blitzkrieg raged
And the bodies stank

(Refrain)

I shouted out,
"Who killed the Kennedys?"
When after all
It was you and me

Just as every cop is a criminal
And all the sinners, saints
As heads is tails, just call me Lucifer
'Cause I'm in need of some restraint[141]

"Sympathy for the Devil" is a remarkable piece of work to have entered popular culture at a time when most other musicians were singing about surfboards, pretty girls and fast cars. Presented from the point of view of Satan, it boasts of the devil's hellish accomplishments and gloats over mankind's complicity in the demonic plan. Several points about the song are obviously pertinent to the view outlined earlier. First, during the two thousand years that passed between the Passion of Christ and the death of Czar Nicholas II, the devil makes no claim of significant involvement in human history.

It is only after the murder of the czar, an act for which Lucifer claims personal responsibility, that his puzzling "game" gets under way. Once the Czar was killed and "Anastasia screamed in vain," this demon is immersed in international war, civil strife, intra-

---

[141] Copyright Mick Jagger and Keith Richards.

personal hatred and every form of godlessness that can be mentioned in a few short verses. One senses he is no mere participant, but rather the cause of these atrocities. He is even behind the cultural redefining, or should we say un-defining, of values. Under his influence black becomes white and wrong becomes right, as "heads is tails."

The last line of these lyrics is most revealing, for here Lucifer admits that his "withholding one" is gone. Whatever kept the devil in check from the time of Christ until the czar's death has been removed, and he mockingly claims to be "in need of some restraint." We would say that the withholding one was Roman Christian monarchy, whose final representative was Czar Nicholas II.

About this, Mr. Jenkins writes, "I believe strongly that the song 'Sympathy for the Devil' is one of those things that God permits to occur to warn the faithful as to the 'signs of the times.' As our Lord said, 'when you see that the tree is green, then know that the time draweth nigh.' ... Why would Mick Jagger put this emphasis into this song, if it was just his own idea to write it? This song can provide those who are attentive with some insight into what is going on and has been going on since that terrible night in 1918."

The Short Reign of Antichrist

The "falling away" of mankind's faith when confronted with evil of immense proportions—this may well be the object of Satan's "game." And it is expected to reach epidemic proportions prior to Antichrist's actual appearance since the Scriptures indicate that he will not have much time to achieve his diabolical ends. "After that he must be loosed a little season," writes St. John (Rev. 20:3). This little season of Satan's freedom is believed to corresponds to the short time allowed the devil on earth: "Woe to the inhabiters of the earth and of the sea! For the devil is come down unto you, having great wrath, because he knoweth that he hath but a short time" (Rev. 12:12).

The Lord tells us that this period is kept brief so that every living creature will not be killed off by Antichrist's rage: "And except those days should be shortened, there should no flesh be saved: but for the elect's sake those days shall be shortened" (Mat. 24:22). It will be a time of unprecedented suffering, that the Lord in His compassion will not prolong, as St. John Chrysostom says, "For if the Jewish war was shortened for the elect's sake, much more shall this tribulation be shortened for these same's sake."[142]

Still, when someone is suffering, a second or a minute can seem like eternity. In addition the psalmist says, "a thousand years in thy sight are but as yesterday when it is past, and as a watch in the night" (Psalm 90:4). Therefore, what God calls a short time we might regard as interminable. So the question naturally arises, just how short is short?

---

[142] John Chrysostom, *Homilies on the Gospel According to St. Matthew*, LXXVI, 3.

Daniel offers a clue when he speaks of "the prince that shall come," which will destroy the city and the sanctuary. This prince is prophesied to "confirm the covenant with many for one week, and in the midst of the week he shall cause the sacrifice and the oblation to cease, and for the overspreading of abominations he shall make it desolate, even unto the consummation" (Dan. 9:27).

This "week" is composed of years instead of days, and is thought to represent the whole period of Antichrist's operation in the world. Hippolytus says, "For by one week he indicates the showing forth of the seven years which shall be in the last times."[143] "For when Daniel said, 'I shall make my covenant for one week,' he indicated seven years; and the one half of the week is for the preaching of the prophets, and for the other half of the week--that is to say, for three years and a half--Antichrist will reign upon the earth."[144]

Of this week, the second half is to be that period called the Great Tribulation. During this time, Antichrist is expected to abandon his humanitarian guise and exercise all the devilish powers at his command. So important is this period that Daniel speaks of it more than once in coded form and using the word "time," to represent a year: "They [the saints] shall be given into his [Antichrist's] hand until a time and times and the dividing of time" (Dan. 7:25). "Time" equals one year, "times" equals two years, and "the dividing of time"

---

[143] Hippolytus, *Appendix to the Works of Hippolytus*, XXI.

[144] Hippolytus, *Appendix to the Works of Hippolytus*, XXV.

equals half a year. Add these together to make three and one half years.

Elsewhere this is expressed even more clearly: "It shall be for a time, times and an half; and when he [Antichrist] shall have accomplished to scatter the power of the holy people, all these things shall be finished" (Dan. 12:7). We find this same coded reference in the Book of Revelation describing the period in which the Church, as represented by the woman giving birth, is protected from the dragon: "And to the woman were given two wings of a great eagle, that she might fly into the wilderness, into her place, where she is nourished for a time, and times, and half a time, from the face of the serpent" (Rev. 12:14).

Victorinus writes, "The little season signifies three years and six months, in which with all his power the devil will avenge himself through Antichrist against the Church."[145] St. Augustine concurs with this assessment: "But when the short time comes he shall be loosed. For he shall rage with the whole force of himself and his angels for three years and six months; and those with whom he makes war shall have power to withstand all his violence and stratagems."[146]

St. John reveals in his Revelation: "And there was given me a reed like unto a rod: and the angel stood, saying, Rise, and measure the temple of God, and the altar, and them that worship therein. But the court

[145] Victorinus, *Commentary on the Apocalypse of the Blessed John*, XX.

[146] Augustine, *City of God*, XX, 8.

which is without the temple leave out, and measure it not; for it is given unto the Gentiles; and the holy city shall they tread under food forty and two months" (Rev. 11:1-2).

Forty-two months is three and a half years, which is the second half of the seven-year period described in Daniel's week of days. According to Archbishop Averky, "The treading of the Holy City, Jerusalem, or the ecumenical Church for the course of forty-two months signifies that at the coming of Antichrist the faithful will be persecuted for the course of three and a half years."[147]

Job's Temptation and Triumph

In Daniel we read that the saints will be given into Antichrist's hand. Meanwhile, St. Augustine affirms that the Church will have the power to withstand the evil one. How are we to resolve this seeming contradiction? The Book of Job provides instruction and an object lesson on what to expect in the last days, for here we witness a man being tempted directly by Satan.

The story of Job takes place prior to Christ's first advent. This was the period before Satan was bound, where as a strong man in his own house he freely worked evil against mankind. "Now there came a day when the sons of God came to present themselves before the Lord, and Satan came also among them. And the Lord said unto Satan, Whence comest thou? Then

[147] Archbishop Averky Taushev, p. 165.

Satan answered the Lord, and said, from going to and fro in the earth, and from walking up and down in it" (Job 1:6-7).

Satan and the Lord have a conversation in which it is revealed that Job has been shielded from evil — perhaps a figure of the Church's protection during Christ's thousand-year reign. Satan spoke to the Lord as follows: "Doth Job fear God for naught? Hast not thou made an hedge about him, and about his house, and about all that he hath on every side? Thou hast blessed the work of his hands, and his substance is increased in the land. But put forth thine hand now, and touch all that he hath, and he will curse thee to thy face. And the Lord said unto Satan, Behold, all that he hath is in thy power; only upon himself put not forth thine hand" (Job 1:9-12).

Then Satan goes forth and devises evil for Job. His oxen, camels and asses are all stolen, fire from heaven falls upon his sheep. We should notice that God allows Satan to make fire fall from the air — which is his realm, after all — a seemingly miraculous skill which will be utilized in the last days by Antichrist to deceive the masses: "And he doeth great wonders, so that he maketh fire come down from heaven on the earth in the sight of men. And deceiveth them that dwell on the earth by the means of those miracles which he had power to do." (Rev. 13:13-14). About this, Augustine says,

> For when he fell from heaven as fire, and at a stroke swept away from the holy Job his nu-

merous household and his vast flocks, and then as a whirlwind rushed upon and smote the house and killed his children, these were not deceitful appearances, and yet they were the works of Satan to whom God had given this power.[148]

Job's servants are murdered and a tornado blows down the house in which his children are eating. Within minutes, Job is reduced to poverty and destitution, but his response is humble: "Then Job arose, and rent his mantle, and shaved his head, and fell down upon the ground, and worshiped, And said, Naked came I out of my mother's womb, and naked I shall return thither: the Lord gave, and the Lord hath taken away; blessed be the name of the Lord" (Job 1:20-21).

The next time the sons of God present themselves before the Lord, God points out to Satan that Job "holdeth fast his integrity, although thou movedst me against him, to destroy him without cause" (Job 2:3). Satan is not impressed however, and predicts that Job will yet sin if his body suffers. God allows this, and Satan "smote Job with sore boils from the sole of his foot unto his crown" (Job 2:7). But in all his suffering Job retains faith in the Lord: "Shall we receive good at the hand of God," he asks, "and shall we not receive evil?"

Job's thought, expressed even before Jesus Christ's Passion, reveals his belief in the coming Messiah, and in a future resurrection for himself. In this Job prefigures the Church of the end times, unconquered by Satan's

---

[148] Augustine, *City of God*, XX, 19.

torments and persecutions. "If a man die, shall he live again? "Job asks. "All the days of my appointed time will I wait, till my change come. For I know that my redeemer liveth, and that he shall stand at the latter day upon the earth. And though after my skin worms destroy my body, yet in my flesh shall I see God" (Job 14:14, 19:25, 26).

Although the devil exercised some "power" over Job, that is, the ability to wound his outer man, Job never relinquished his own power to choose for the good. As St. Augustine puts it, "For the Almighty does not absolutely seclude the saints from his temptation, but shelters only their inner man, where faith resides, that by outward temptation they may grow in grace."[149]

So also will it be in the last days. Those subject to Antichrist outwardly will retain power to oppose him in their inner man. The choice, however difficult to make under conditions of persecution, will always remain theirs. As Ephraim the Syrian says,

> To men that are just and upright, temptations become helps. Job, a man of discernment, was victorious in temptations. Sickness came upon him and he complained not; disease afflicted him and he murmured not; his body failed and his strength departed, but his will was not weakened. He proved perfect in all by sufferings, for as much as temptations crushed him not.... See then, O thou that art wise, the power

---

[149] Augustine, *City of God*, XX, 8.

that freedom possesses; that nothing can injure it unless the will is weakened."[150]

The Threat of Deception

Much has been said about the difficulties people are likely to experience in the end times. Indeed, the prospect of avoiding these is one of the main appeals of the rapture theory. But loving this life too much makes one especially vulnerable to Antichrist. As St. John Chrysostom says,

> Even if we do not choose to suffer any of the things that are painful for Christ's sake, we must in other ways most assuredly endure them. For neither, though thou shouldest not have died for Christ, wilt thou be immortal; neither though thou shouldest not have cast away thy riches for Christ, wilt thou go away hence with them. He willeth thee to do these by choice, which thou must do by necessity. So much only he requires to be added, that it be done for his sake. Seest thou how easy the conflict?[151]

What threat then does Antichrist hold? As Satan tempted Job, so is it likely that Antichrist will tempt the Christians of the last days, for the Lord says: "For in

---

[150] Ephraim the Syrian, *On Admonition and Repentance,* XX.

[151] John Chrysostom, *Homilies on the Gospel According to St. Matthew,* LXXVI, 4.

those days shall be affliction, such as was not from the beginning of the creation which God created unto this time, neither shall be" (Mark 13:19). Like Decius, Diocletian and other God-haters, Antichrist is expected to torment Christians. But the devils, according to John of Damascus, "have no power or strength against any one except what God in His dispensation hath conceded to them, as for instance, against Job and those swine that are mentioned in the Gospels."[152]

Consequently Antichrist will have no power to compel a human soul to evil, any more than the serpent could force Eve to eat the forbidden fig in the Garden of Eden. The martyred and persecuted Christians of the end times will retain free will always. The real threat which Antichrist poses is much more subtle than merely creating misery — it is deception.

Jesus does not warn us to horde food, nor to stockpile provisions — quite the opposite, for He says, "take no thought for your life, what ye shall eat or what ye shall drink" (Mat. 6:25). But we *are* supposed to be careful about being deceived: "Take heed that ye be not deceived," says He, "for many will come in my name, saying I am Christ" (Luke 21:8). Of course, Antichrist will be the chief of all those pretenders.

We are not to be anxious about everyday needs, but we *are* to be anxious about being tricked by Antichrist. Why? In the first place, because most people *will* be deceived, and peer pressure to believe what is false will be

---

[152] John of Damascus, *An Exact Exposition of the Orthodox Faith,* II, 30.

intense. Also, mere human resources will avail little against the great deceiver whose coach is the father of lies. He who was able to tempt sinless Eve will have no difficulty tempting Eve's children. Those who are deceived will believe. They will accept wrong for right, false for true. "'For they shall show signs and wonders, so as to deceive the very elect,'" St. John Chrysostom elucidates the Lord's words:

> Here he is speaking of Antichrist, and see how he secures them: "Go not forth into the deserts, enter not into the secret chambers." He did not say, "Go, and do not believe;" but, "Go not forth, neither depart thither." For great then will be the deceiving, because that even deceiving miracles are wrought.[153]

Does He Know You?

If believing in Christ is sufficient to save the soul, then believing in Antichrist may be sufficient to damn it. Therefore we must believe in Christ, and not believe in Antichrist. For, "believing in" someone is not at all the same as merely believing that someone is. Even if we confidently believe that God exists, such faith is not adequate to secure our salvation, as St. James points out: "Thou believest that there is one God; thou doest well. The devils also believe, and tremble" (James 2:19). We must not only believe that Christ is, we must be-

---

[153] John Chrysostom, *Homilies on the Gospel According to St. Matthew*, LXXVI, 2.

lieve *in* Christ, for in this way we enter into personal relationship with our Lord: "Ye believe in God, believe also in me" (John 14:1). At the moment of trial mental convictions may fall away, but a living relationship with God will sustain us.

The hope of Christians is to belong to Christ's kingdom in its earthly manifestation, that is, the Church, and to enter after death into Christ's eternal kingdom. The Lord warns us that lip service is not enough to achieve this: "Not everyone that saith unto me, Lord, Lord, shall enter into the kingdom of heaven, but he that doeth the will of my Father, who is in heaven. Many will say to me in that day, Lord, Lord, have we not prophesied in thy name. And in thy name have cast out demons? And in thy name done many wonderful works? And then I will profess unto them, I never knew you; depart from me, ye that work iniquity" (Mat. 7:21-23).

What is doing the Father's will? Obviously it is the opposite of working iniquity. We are to do godly works, or better still, the work of God. Jesus says, "This is the work of God, that ye believe on him whom he hath sent" (John 6:29). The work of God is, paradoxically, to be in relationship with our Lord Jesus, to believe in Him.

If our knowledge of God is no more than mental conceptions, then we do not know Him, and presumably, He does not know us. Having ideas is not enough. Even prophesying and doing wonderful works in His name is not enough. We must be in relationship with the Lord and live *in* Him, as St. John says, "And now little children, abide in him; that, when he shall appear, we may have confidence, and not be ashamed before him at his coming" (1 John 2:28).

How do we find the Lord to be in relationship with Him? Jesus speaks of giving food to the hungry, drink to the thirsty, a home to strangers, clothing to the naked, visits to the sick and imprisoned. This is the way to the kingdom of heaven, for He says, "Inherit the kingdom prepared for you from the foundation of the world, for . . . inasmuch as ye have done it unto one of the least of these my brethren, ye have done it unto me" (Mat. 25:34, 40).

CHAPTER NINE

The Rapture:
When Will I Be Free?

Once Jonathan Kalgari's business took him to the city convention center while a conference was in progress there on the subject of the end times. As he drove into the parking lot, he noticed that many cars had bumper stickers reading, "Warning! In case of rapture this car will be left driverless."

John pondered this scenario as he walked into the center. He visualized people floating up from the freeway, executives waving briefcases and truckers still clutching CB radio microphones, while their abandoned vehicles careened wildly or, (with God's merciful intervention) coasted safely to a stop. John imagined the sky gradually filling with the gently ascending, cheering bodies of Christians, while those left behind stared dumbfounded, anxious and resentful.

A question about this whole idea nagged at Jonathan. As he left the center and drove out of the parking lot, he noticed a group of demonstrators standing by the road. They were a diverse group, some a bit shaggy, others rather upscale. But they all had signs with the same words printed on them. "Guess they are wondering the same thing as me," mused Jonathan, and read out loud: "In case of rapture, can I have your car?"

There is no documented evidence of discord among patristic writers concerning the revealed events of the Lord's return. Even those few who believed Christ's second coming would precede His thousand year reign, such as Lactantius and Irenaeus, never suggested that the rapture of Christians would occur anytime other than at the Lord's glorious appearing. Lactantius says that God "will immediately send a deliverer. Then the middle of the heaven shall be laid open in the dead and darkness of the night, that the light of the descending God may be made manifest in all the world as lightning."[154]

Following with more detail, Hippolytus says,

> These things, then, being come to pass, beloved, and the one week being divided into two parts, and the abomination of desolation being manifested then, and the two prophets and forerunners of the Lord having finished their course, and the whole world finally approaching the consummation, what remains but the coming of our Lord and Saviour Jesus Christ from heaven, for whom we have looked in hope?[155]

Belief that Christ will raise up believers at His second coming (Greek *parousia*) is fundamental to Christian thought, since St. Paul describes the event in Holy Scripture:

[154] Lactantius, *The Divine Institutes,* Book 7, IX.
[155] Hippolytus, *Works of Hippolytus,* II, 64.

For the Lord himself shall descend from heaven with a shout, with the voice of the archangel, and with the trump of God: and the dead in Christ shall rise first: Then we which are alive and remain shall be caught up together with them in the clouds, to meet the Lord in the air: and so shall we ever be with the Lord (1 Thes. 4:16-17).

St. John Chrysostom attempted to visualize how that scene should appear:

Let us represent then in word that this is now present. For if sudden death, or earthquakes in cities, and threatenings thus terrify our souls; when we see the earth breaking up, and crowded with all these, when we hear the trumpets, and the voice of the Archangel louder than any trumpet, when we perceive the heaven shriveled up, and God the King of all himself coming nigh --what then will be our souls? Let us shudder, I beseech you, and be frightened as if these things were now taking place. Let us not comfort ourselves by the delay. For when it must certainly happen, the delay profits us nothing."[156]

St. Paul also describes the event thus: "Behold, I show you a mystery; we shall not all sleep, but we shall all be changed, in a moment, in the twinkling of an eye, at the last trump: for the trumpet shall sound, and the

[156] John Chrysostom, *On Paul to the Thessalonians*, VIII.

dead shall be raised incorruptible, and we shall be changed" (1 Cor. 15:51-52). From these passages the rapture can be understood not so much as a physical experience, but rather as an instantaneous spiritual transformation—or resurrection, as St. John Chrysostom calls it.[157]

Modern Rapture

Although belief in Parousia is implicit in the canonical Scriptures, the rapture as described by premillennialists is a novelty of comparatively modern making, popularized most by John Darby of the "Plymouth" Brethren in Great Britain. Even Protestant scholars admit the idea dates to no earlier than the nineteenth century. "It is true that the pre-Trib position was not formed until 1826-28," concedes LaHaye.

There is an appeal associated with developing new insights and interpretations, and the prophetic writings of the Bible offering plenty of scope for the fertile imagination to run riot. G. K. Chesterton once made the pithy observation that "though St. John the Evangelist saw many strange monsters in his vision, he saw no creature as wild as one of his commentators."[158]

This rapture concept is a byproduct of a system of Biblical hermeneutics and philosophy called "dispensationalism." Dispensationalists believe that the prophecies concerning Israel will yet be fulfilled in the

---

[157] John Chysostom, *Homilies on the Gospel According to St. Matthew*, LXXVI, 5.

[158] G. K. Chesterton, *Orthodoxy*, II, p. 17.

last days, and that the Scriptures can only be understood properly by separating the prophecies concerning the Church from those concerning the Jews. Dispensationalists also reject the Holy Church as an institution of tradition and sacraments, and define the "church" as only "that body of believers who found Christ through faith, and they alone would pass through the final judgment and enter into eternal life."[159]

Dispensationalism has taken the rapture out of context of Christ's Second Coming and imagined it as a distinct event occurring years earlier. Since this scenario postulates a miraculous event occurring in the middle of otherwise normal times, fantastic images result. Cars and planes are left without people to drive or pilot them as people suddenly disappear from the face of the earth. "A million conversations will end midsentence," fantasizes Tim LaHaye.

A million phone receivers will suddenly go dead. A woman will reach for a man's hand in the dark . . . and no one will be there. A man will turn with a laugh to slap a colleague on the back and his hand will move through empty air. A basketball player will make a length-of-the-floor pass to a teammate streaking down-court and find there is no one there to receive it. And no referee to call out-of-bounds. A mother will pull back the covers in a bassinet, smelling the sweet baby smell one moment but suddenly

[159] Clouse, Hosack & Pierard, *The New Millennium Manual* (Grand Rapids MI: Baker Books, 1999), p. 94.

kissing empty space and looking into empty blankets."[160]

The Secret Rapture

The main contention surrounding the rapture is not so much about how it will happen however, but when. St. Paul clearly indicates that the Parousia is associated with the Lord's second coming, and Orthodoxy affirms that these two events will be virtually simultaneous. That is, when the Lord returns in glory, the trumpet will sound and the dead in Christ will arise from their graves. Then the living Christians will join together with these formerly dead souls to meet the Lord "in the air." Since the Lord's coming in glory must follow on the heels of the Great Tribulation, it is evident that "we which are alive and remain," as St. Paul puts it, are those Christians who have survived during the reign of Antichrist. And indeed even the tenor of this phrase "we who are alive and remain" suggests just that— those who are left among the living after the terrors of the end times.

On the other hand, Premillennialists insist that they do not deserve to be present during the last days. "The hope and comfort of the Rapture demands that we escape the Tribulation," says LaHaye, "being raptured out of this world before God's wrath begins."[161] In order to "escape the Tribulation," they first postulate that the

---

[160] Tim LaHaye, *Rapture*, p. 40.
[161] Tim LaHaye, *Rapture*, p. 68.

rapture will actually occur *before* the tribulation (those subscribing to this notion are called "pre-Trib"). In other words, they set the date of rapture fully seven years earlier than the Lord's glorious appearing in power.

Next, they say that this coming of the Lord to rapture His Christians will be a secret event known only to the believers themselves: "Jesus said His coming will be exactly like that," exults Hal Lindsey in reference to Noah. "But—which coming? His secret coming for the Church, or His coming in power and glory at the end of the Tribulation? In the Rapture, only the Christians see Him—it's a mystery, a secret."[162]

Although the modern conception of rapture is less than 150 years old, patristic writers from the first few centuries of the Church spoke out vigorously against any suggestion that Christ would return secretly. They warn us that the Lord's Second Coming will be a worldwide event. "The true Christ, the Only-begotten Son of God, comes no more from the earth," declares St. Cyril of Jerusalem. "Look no longer downwards and to the earth; for the Lord descends from heaven; not alone as before, but with many, escorted by tens of thousands of Angels; *nor secretly* as the dew on the fleece; but shining forth openly as the lightning."[163]

The Lord Himself instructs us not to look for Him in obscure places. He may come unexpectedly, but His

---

[162] Hal Lindsey, *There's a New World Coming,* p. 62, 131.
[163] Cyril of Jerusalem, *Catechetical Lectures*, XV, 10.

coming will certainly not be hidden. Indeed, it will be impossible for anyone to be unaware of it.

> Then, if any man shall say unto you, Lo, here is Christ, or there; believe it not: for there shall arise false Christs, and false prophets, and shall show signs and wonders, so as to deceive, if possible, the very elect. Behold, I have told you before. Wherefore if they shall say unto you, Behold, He is in the desert, go not forth: behold, He is in the secret chambers, believe it not. For as the lightning cometh out of the east, and shineth even unto the west, so shall also the coming of the Son of Man be. For wheresoever the carcass is, there shall the eagles be gathered together (Mat. 24:23-28).

Lindsey's description of a so-called "secret coming" reveals both ignorance of patristic testimony and willingness to manipulate Scripture. From out of nowhere, three comings of the Lord have been conjured: His first, in humility; His third, in glory; and His second, in *secrecy!* And this is despite the Lord's own clear direction that He will not be found in a secret place. There is no question among the fathers about how many times Jesus comes to earth. "He speaks here of two appearings," says St. John Chrysostom of Paul's letter to Titus, "for there are two; the first of grace, the second of retribution and justice."[164]

---

[164]John Chrysostom, *Homilies on the Epistle of St. Paul to Titus*, I.

Stung by the accusation that they have created a third coming of the Lord when the Scriptures provide for only two, some premillennialists retain their timing of the rapture but explain that instead of two second comings, there is to be one long, drawn out one—lasting over seven years! It is supposed to begin prior to the Great Tribulation with a "rapture phase" and conclude after it with a "Glorious Appearing phase." According to LaHaye, "the Glorious Appearing is the literal, physical stage of His Second Coming, the coming of the church to the earth. The Rapture is His return for the church."[165]

Yet how can this be justified when the Scriptures teach that the Lord's Second Coming will be instantaneous, "in a moment, in the twinkling of an eye?" The Gospel and Epistles alike leave no room for doubt that the whole process will be "as the lightning," that is, faster than the mind of man can comprehend. Lightning is a strong image, for it is blinding, instantaneous light. Yet it is near at hand—not like the sun, whose rays come across the universe and bathe the earth east to west in equal amounts of light. The Lord will arrive as lightning—he will proceed from a certain place in which His light will go forth announcing his presence throughout the world. St. John Chrysostom writes,

> For not, as when at His former coming He appeared in Bethlehem, and in a small corner of the world, and no one knew Him at the beginning, so doth He say it shall be then too; but

[165]Tim LaHaye, *Rapture*, p. 79.

openly and with all circumstance, and so as not to need one to tell these things. And this is no small sign that *He will not come secretly*. Having told them how Antichrist cometh, as, for instance, that it will be in a place; He saith how Himself also cometh. How then doth He Himself come? "As the lightning cometh out of the east, and shineth even unto the west, so shall also the coming of the Son of Man be."[166]

The Blessed Hope

Because there is so little in St. Paul's account of our Lord's Second Coming to support the premillennialist rapture view, other Scriptures have been combed for useful phrases. One of the most promising was found in St. Paul's letter to Titus:

> For the grace of God that bringeth salvation hath appeared to all men, teaching us that, denying ungodliness and worldly lusts, we should live soberly, righteously, and godly, in this present world. Looking for that blessed hope, and the glorious appearing of the great God and our Savior, Jesus Christ (Tit 2:11-13).

By isolating verse thirteen from the surrounding passages, premillennialists infer in the words "blessed hope" a reference to their rapture, simply because it

[166] John Chrysostom, *Homilies on the Gospel According to St. Matthew*, LXXVI, 2.

appears in the same sentence as the words "glorious appearing." LaHaye is not embarrassed to claim that, "Paul's 'blessed hope' is the Rapture, for it is unique to the church. No one else will take part in it."[167]

St. John Chrysostom emphasizes that the Lord's second coming will be a blessing beyond words, yet he by no means suggests that "blessed hope" should be understood as the rapture alone, or indeed a particular aspect of Christ's return, but rather the fullness of that wondrous event: "For nothing is more blessed and more desirable than that appearing. Words are not able to represent it, the blessings thereof surpass our understanding."[168]

Reading the passage for its plainest sense (which Bible literalists claim to do), and in the context of the surrounding verses, a more appropriate interpretation can easily be seen. In verse twelve St. Paul describes the Christian standards by which we are to live in *this world*. We are to deny ungodliness and worldly lusts, and live soberly, righteously and godly. We are to do this in order to acquire "that blessed hope." Since this is no ordinary or pragmatic hope but rather a blessed one, it must be for what is very wonderful indeed. But what would that be?

In order to determine to what blessed hope St. Paul refers, it is instructive to note that there are only a handful of passages in the Bible—even in the most liberal of interpretations—that can be thought to reference the

[167] Tim LaHaye, *Rapture*, p. 68.
[168] John Chrysostom, *Homilies on the Epistle of Paul to Titus*, I.

resurrection (or rapture) of believers at the Lord's Second Coming. The rapture is a one-time event, after all, and even then only part of the larger and vastly more important occasion of our Lord's Return.

On the other hand, there are five hundred and fifty references to "heaven" in the Bible. So significant is this topic that Jesus began His public ministry with the words, "Repent ye, for the kingdom of heaven is at hand" (Mat. 3:2). Indeed, His entire life and ministry revolved around this theme. Through His death and resurrection, Christ opened the way to heaven, which had been closed since Adam. He made a way for mankind to return to the Father. He obliterated the necessity of death and the claim of hell. As a result of all this, ETERNAL LIFE is possible to human souls, and this is the biggest news and the vastest hope in the universe!

Compare St. Paul's "blessed hope" to his two other references to hope in the same letter to Titus. In both cases he identifies hope in the strongest terms not with a particular event (such as rapture), but with eternal life in heaven. We are to live, he says, "in *hope of eternal life,* which God, that cannot lie, promised before the world began" (Tit.1:20). "That being justified by his grace, we should be made heirs according to the *hope of eternal life*" (Tit. 3:7).

From this alone we can see that forcing St. Paul's "blessed hope" to refer to the premillennialist rapture is a stretch of immense proportions. In fact, this term "blessed hope" appears nowhere else in the entire Bible. The only other place where the words "blessed" and "hope" can even be found in the same passage is in

First Peter, where Christian hope is again directed where it should be — toward heaven:

> Blessed be the God and Father of our Lord Jesus Christ, which according to his abundant mercy hath begotten us again to a lively *hope* by the resurrection of Jesus Christ from the dead, to an inheritance incorruptible, and undefiled, and that fadeth not away, reserved *in heaven* for you (1 Pet. 1:3-4).

Clearly, the hope, and especially the blessed hope, of Christians is that of entering the heavenly kingdom in the *world to come*. What higher thing could possibly be hoped for? Life eternal with Jesus is the universal aspiration of the human soul. Ultimately, nothing matters more than being reunited with God in the kingdom of heaven.

Thief in the Night

In Revelations chapter 16, between the sixth and seventh "vial judgments," we hear the Lord, say, "Behold, I come as a thief. Blessed is he that watcheth, and keepeth his garments, lest he walk naked, and they see his shame" (Rev. 16:15). Premillennialists have used this metaphor of the Lord's coming as a thief to promote their idea of a secret return of Christ for Christians. Hal Lindsey writes that there are "*two stages* in Jesus' second coming. One passage of Scripture speaks of Christ's coming *in the air* and in *secret*, like a thief coming in the night. Another part of the Scripture describes

Christ's coming in power and majesty *to the earth,* with *every eye* seeing him."[169]

However, an examination of the "thief in the night" theme elsewhere in the Bible indicates that premillennialists are missing the point. It is not that the Lord will be secretive and unseen, but rather that a sleeping world will fail to notice His arrival. The colossal events of the Second Coming will appear suddenly and without warning to those who haven't been paying attention. Noah built his ark in plain view, and was a hundred years in doing it, but only he and his family were prepared when the rains started. Everyone else was caught by surprise.

How secret will it be when the heavens pass away with a great noise? How about when the earth is burning with fervent heat? But St. Peter links these dramatic events specifically to the Lord's coming as a thief in the night: "But the day of the Lord will come as a thief in the night, in the which the heavens shall pass away with a great noise, and the elements shall melt with fervent heart, the earth also and the works that are therein shall be burned up" (2 Peter 3:10).

The day of the Lord has been prophesied for millennia, and yet it will come as a shock to sinful man precisely because his attention is not on God. We are warned to "watch" not because Christ's return will be an easily missed secret event, but because it will catch off guard those who trust in this world for their security. "For you yourselves know perfectly that the day of

---

[169] Hal Lindsey, *There's A New World Coming,* p. 61.

the Lord so cometh as a thief in the night," warns St. Paul. "For when they shall say, Peace and safety, then sudden destruction cometh upon them"(1 Thes. 5:2-3).

And finally, St. Paul concludes with an admonition that should forever end the debate on this issue. So far from applying the idea that the Lord comes to them in some secret way, St. Paul affirms that His coming should *never* be to them as a thief in the night! "But ye, brethren, are not in the darkness, that that day should overtake you as a thief" (1 Thes. 5:4).

The Thief Who Robs Satan

Recall that Jesus also characterized Himself as a thief with regard to spoiling Satan's house at His first coming (see chapter three, "The Strong Man's House"). "If the Goodman of the house had known what hour the thief would come, he would have watched, and not have suffered his house to be broken through. Be ye therefore ready also: for the Son of man cometh at an hour when ye think not" (Luke 12:39). At the Lord's first coming Satan was loose, and at His second coming Satan will again be loose. Jesus thus serves notice that He will surprise even the Devil, and will certainly surprise all those who allow the devil to influence their lives.

The Messiah had long been prophesied to come to the Jews. And even though their Scriptures revealed where He would be born they still missed Him. Such will also be the fate in the last days of many who consider themselves Christians. They have the warnings of

187

Scripture bidding them watch, but will they be ready? "'That that Day,' he says, 'may not overtake you as a thief,'" says St. John Chrysostom. "For in the case of those who are watching and who are in the light, if there should be any entry of a robber, it can do them no harm: so also it is with those who live well. But those who are sleeping he will strip of everything, and go off; that is, those who are trusting in the things of this life."[170]

In the last days the Lord promises to come as a thief in the night, and many will be spiritually sleeping at that time. However momentous the events of the end times, their real significance will not even be comprehended by those whose minds are far from God: "Antichrist indeed shall appear, after whom is the end, and the punishments at the end, and vengeance intolerable; but they that are held by the intoxication of wickedness shall not so much as perceive the dreadful nature of the things that are on the point of being done."[171]

As stated earlier, Noah prefigured the end times. He spent a century building the ark. It was a huge project that couldn't be hidden, and his neighbors had plenty of opportunity to prepare themselves as Noah was doing. But their faith was in the world, and when the rains came their earthly refuges fell apart. Consequently, the ark is a metaphor for the Church,

[170] John Chrysostom, *Homilies on the Gospel According to St. Matthew*, LXXVII, 2.
[171] John Chrysostom, *Homilies on the Gospel According to St. Matthew*, LXXVII, 2.

preserving Christians from the flood that destroys all others. About this, St. John Chrysostom says,

> How then does Jesus say "after the tribulation of those days?" If there be luxury, how is there tribulation? Luxury for them that are in a state of insensibility and peace. Therefore he said not, when there is peace, but "when they speak of peace and safety," indicating that their insensibility to be such as those in Noah's time, for that amid such evils they lived in luxury. When Antichrist is come, the pursuit of unlawful pleasures shall be more eager among the transgressors. For like as when the ark was making, they believed not, saith He; but while it was set in the midst of them, proclaiming beforehand the evils that are to come, they, when they saw it, lived in pleasure, just as though nothing dreadful were about to take place."[172]

Preparation

How do we watch for Christ and prepare for Antichrist? Is it a matter of remaining in a state of agitation about the sinful nature of the world and its accelerating descent towards Hell? The Scriptures tell us that these negative things don't need our attention. If Noah thought about his soon-to-be-dead neighbors, the fact is not recorded in Scripture and probably didn't distract

[172] John Chrysostom, *Homilies on the Gospel According to St. Matthew*, LXXVII, 2.

him much. He did think about God, however, for that was what counted. We also must think about God and what God wants of us.

A certain man was asked what he would do if he knew the world would end the following day. "I would cultivate my garden," he replied calmly.

Even so, the events of the end times or any other times are incidental when our attention is properly placed on God. Christians should always be in a state of preparation, and whether they are living in last days or not should make little difference in their outlook and behavior. Our main concern should be to tend the garden, which is a good metaphor for the work of uprooting sins and helping virtues to grow. St. Paul spelled out a succinct plan for this in the Titus text cited earlier: "Denying ungodliness and worldly lusts, we should live soberly, righteously, and godly, in this present world."

Such preparation should be ongoing whether or not the Tribulation lies directly ahead. Indeed the actual performance of these is what separates real saints from nominal Christians, enabling them to live even in this present life as though already in heaven. Anyone whose inner life is thus ordered need have no fear of Antichrist, for he has defeated Satan in his own heart and mind already.

Preparation is clearly a weak spot in the premillennialist perspective, however. Not wanting to face the Tribulation, they can scarcely justify getting ready for it. The very idea stumps LaHaye, who can conceive of nothing beyond memorizing Bible verses: "How could one prepare for such a time of Tribulation? True, we could memorize more Scripture..."[173]

Evil cannot be resisted, nor God loved, through mere intellectual processes. Among the Russian martyrs of the twentieth century it was noted that when believers were sent to Communist prisons for their convictions, academics and seminarians were always the first to yield to torture and implicate their comrades. On the other hand, there were many simple Orthodox Christians who, because of their heartfelt faith in God and refusal to deny Christ, were kept in solitary confinement for many years. After a long time of such punishment, one poor sufferer found that he could no longer remember the Scriptural passages he once knew so well. Gradually even the Lord's Prayer was obliterated from his persecuted awareness, and all that remained was the feeling in his heart that God was real. Yet this powerful awareness, beyond all mental concepts and convictions, enabled him to survive with sanity and faith intact.

The Chosen and the Elect

Premillennialists claim that only unbelievers will be left behind after all the Christians are raptured into heaven. These people, consisting of both Jews and Gentiles, will be the ones to personally experience the troubles of the end times. God's purpose in removing Christians from the earth (aside from their not "need-

[173] Tim LaHaye, *Rapture*, p. 70.

ing" it because they have been good) is so He can concentrate on fulfilling ancient prophecies to Israel. "There is a distinction between God's purpose for the nation of Israel and His purpose for the church, which is His main program today," says Lindsey. Since the Church has already demonstrated its allegiance to Christ, the "time of tribulation... seems to be a resumption of God's dealing with Israel."[174]

According to the dispensational model, not only the tribulation but also Christ's return in glory is reserved for unbelieving Jews and Gentiles. "The glorious appearing," says LaHaye, "is not for the Christian but for the remnant at the end of the Tribulation. It will primarily affect the Jews and those who have been good to them, who somehow survive the Tribulation."[175]

As premillennialists pride themselves on taking the meaning of the Scriptures literally, let us inquire into the Bible on these points. First, to whom is St. Paul speaking when he says, "teaching *us* that . . . *we* should... [be] looking for... the glorious appearing of the great God and our Savior, Jesus Christ" (Tit. 2:11)? Is he speaking to recalcitrant Jews and unbelieving Gentiles? Or is he speaking to Christians about Christians?

Consider an even stronger passage: "What is our hope, or joy, or crown of rejoicing?" St. Paul asks the Christians of Thessaloniki. "Are not even ye in the presence of our Lord at his coming?" (1 Thes. 2:19). The answer to his question might also be phrased as "Is [our

---

[174] Hal Lindsey, *The Late Great Planet Earth,* p. 131.
[175] Tim LaHaye, *Rapture,* p. 69.

hope, joy and crown] not that you will be in the presence of our Lord at His coming?" What clearer indication could there be that the Apostles fully expected Christians to be on hand at the Lord's glorious appearing?

And what has the Lord Himself to say about who shall be present during the tribulation and His second coming? "For in those days shall be affliction, such as was not from the beginning of the creation which God created unto this time, neither shall be. And except the Lord had shortened those days, no flesh should be saved; but for the elect's sake, whom he hath chosen, he hath shortened the days" (Mark 13: 19-20). Jesus emphasizes that those hard times will be shortened *for no other reason* than that His elect, whom He has chosen, will be enduring them.

And who are these elect whom the Lord has chosen? The premillennialists will claim that they are Jews, but does this accord with Scripture? "You have not chosen me, but I have chosen you out of the world," said Jesus to His disciples (John 15:16). Nor were His words for them alone, but to all Christians who will follow them: "What I say unto you I say unto all..." (Mark 13:37).

"I know whom I have chosen" (John 13:18). Does this simply mean that Jesus can recall the ones he picked out to be His disciples in the same way we might say, "I know what I did yesterday?" There is certainly a deeper meaning, which may be that the Lord is in relationship with each person that He has chosen.

He knows them, and (to a lesser degree) they know Him as well.

> Henceforth I call you not servants; for the servant knoweth not what his lord doeth: but I have called you friends; for all things that I have heard of my father I have made known unto you. *Ye have not chosen me, but I have chosen you,* and ordained you, that you should go and bring forth fruit, and that your fruit should remain (John 15:15-16).

Could anyone disagree that when Christ speaks of His "chosen" he means those Christians whom He has called into His work, from Apostolic times unto the end of the world? St. John spells it out dramatically: "He is Lord of lords, and King of kings, and they that are with Him are called, and chosen, and faithful" (Rev. 17:14). Those that are *with* Christ are His chosen ones.

If the "chosen" are Christians, the "elect" must also be Christians, a conclusion that the Scriptures easily justify. "Put on therefore, as the elect of God" (Col. 3:12), says St. Paul in speaking with Christian disciples. St. Peter likewise calls Christians by this term: "Elect according to the foreknowledge" (1 Pet. 1:12). Jesus warns of those who will try to deceive the elect: "False Christs and false prophets shall arise, and shall show signs and wonders, to seduce, if it were possible, the very elect" (Mark 13:22). These elect cannot possibly refer to the Jews, who in the end times are prophesied to be so *completely* deceived as to make a covenant with Antichrist and consider him their Messiah! "For if he comes to the Jews as Christ, and desires to be worshiped by the Jews, he will make great account of the temple, that he may more completely beguile them."[176]

St. John Chrysostom absolutely declares that it is Christians and not Jews who are the elect. Jews were indeed the elect once—but no more. "You see how at the beginning he sets forth the difference of grace. They are not the elect, but we. For if they were once called the elect, yet are they no longer called so."[177] Therefore the elect are Christians who were chosen *by* God, and who have chosen *for* God. And with this understood, the Lord's own words reveal a Second Coming sequence totally at odds with the premillennialist picture. For He says that the elect will be gathered from the four winds (another way of describing the rapture) *after* the tribulation and *after* the Son of man comes in the clouds!

> But in those days, after that tribulation, the sun shall be darkened, and the moon shall not give its light, and the stars of heaven shall fall, and the powers that are in the heavens shall be shaken. And then shall they see the Son of man coming in the clouds, with great power and glory. And then shall he send his angels, and gather together his elect from the four winds, from the uttermost part of earth to the uttermost part of heaven (Mark 13:24-27).

[176] Cyril of Jerusalem, *Catechetical Lectures*, XV, 14.
[177] John Chrysostom, *Homilies on the Epistle of Paul to Titus*, I.

One can only wonder what kind of Bible LaHaye uses when he makes the incredible assertion that

> no single verse specifically states, "Christ will *not* rapture His church before the Tribulation." On the other hand, no single passage teaches He will not come before the Tribulation, or that He will come in the middle or at the end of the Tribulation. Any such explicit declaration would end the debate immediately. It should also be noted that there is no reference of rapture in connection with the Glorious Appearing.[178]

If any single verse and passage could ever answer such apparent indifference to Biblical truth and integrity, Mark 13:24-27 must be it. For here the rapture is connected with the Glorious Appearing and their exact chronological relationship is laid out: "in *those* days" (the end times), "*after* that tribulation," "*then* they shall see the Son of man coming in the clouds," "and *then* shall he... gather his elect." Seems to this author that the "debate" is over, but then he is not trying to shove a square premillennial stick into the round hole of the Holy Scriptures.

Christians in the Tribulation

These passages leave little room for doubt that Christians will be present during the great tribulation,

---

[178] Tim LaHaye, *Rapture*, p. 180.

and that those who survive those times with faith intact are heaven-bound. "He that shall endure unto the end, the same shall be saved," promises Jesus (Mat. 24:13). Yet premillennialists bemoan this stark fate. "If Christ does not rapture His church before the Tribulation begins, much of the hope is destroyed, and thus it becomes a 'blasted hope.'"[179]

The real problem may be, however, that premillennialists are actually hoping for something other than God's will. Peter was the first of the Apostles to understand that Jesus was Christ, but even so, when the Lord told His disciples that He would go to Jerusalem, suffer and be killed, Peter railed against the idea. "Be it far from thee, Lord," he cried. "This shall not be unto thee" (Mat. 16:22).

Peter's human aversion to pain and suffering kept him from seeing that the Lord welcomed His Cross. We seek comfort and safety at our eternal peril, for these are what the world craves. Peter had his shortcomings, but it is only in this case—in which self-interest hid behind his supposed concerned for Jesus' welfare—that the Lord was so offended as to call Peter Satan! "Get thee behind me, Satan: thou art an offense unto me: for thou savourest not the things that be of God, but those that be of men" (Mat. 16:23).

Why is it necessary for Christians to endure difficulties? In the first place, there is a mystery about suffering which is bound up with God's limitless love. It is therefore inscrutable to our limited understanding.

[179] Tim LaHaye, *Rapture*, p. 69.

Archimandrite Seraphim Aleksiev, who personally suffered under Communism in Bulgaria, wrote,

> We cannot be saved without suffering; how else could we be tested by God for being firm and unwavering in virtue? God arranges many things in life in such a way that man is tempted, so that his free will can be manifested, and he, through the enduring of all trials, can receive salvation. "Because those," according to the words of St. Macarius the Great, "who live in suffering and temptations and endure to the end will not lose the Kingdom of Heaven."[180]

Yet the troubles of the end times are supposed to be greater than those of all previous times. St. Cyril of Jerusalem says of this that the difficulties of the last days present a unique blessing. Because the struggle will be so great, those who endure shall receive a comparably greater reward.[181]

According to St. Augustine, the Tribulation Christians are to be envied above all who have witnessed for Christ:

> And what are we in comparison with those believers and saints who shall then exist, seeing that they shall be tested by the loosing of an en-

---

[180] Archimandrite Seraphim Aleksiev, *The Meaning of Suffering* (Platina, CA: St. Xenia Skete, 1994), p. 51.

[181] Cyril of Jerusalem, *Catechetical Lectures,* XV, 19.

emy with whom we make war at the greatest peril even when he is bound?[182]

But LaHaye persists:

If we locate the Rapture after the Tribulation or in the middle of it, the hope and comfort of the teaching is effectively defaced, particularly once we understand the Tribulation events as ... cataclysms no person can await without dread and dismay. It is a mystery to me how anyone can challenge Christians to live in expectation of the Rapture if it should follow the worst period of God's wrath in history. Can a man honestly get exited about His coming if he knows he can no longer support his family or buy food for them because he refused the mark of the Beast?[183]

There is something of whining in these protestations, not unlike a child crying "unfair!" If, as Orthodox believe, it is God's will that Christians of the end times endure the Great Tribulation, who are we to object? The Lord who allows Christians to experience such an evil day can certainly enable them to live through it (or die in it) triumphantly. For this cause St. Paul counsels us to put on "the whole armor of God, that ye may be able to withstand all in the evil day, and having done all, to stand" (Eph. 6:13).

---

[182] Augustine, *City of God*, XX, 8.
[183] Tim LaHaye, *Rapture*, p. 68.

People have always managed to remain optimistic during dark times, even if they had no idea whether their situation would actually ever improve. But let us try to imagine being alive during the Great Tribulation. What sacrifices might one willingly endure—even embrace—knowing that the Lord was near! Is it conceivable that a Christian could not "get excited about His coming" regardless of what difficulties were to be encountered? Our Lord Himself makes clear that those Christians granted to live during the Great Tribulation should be joyful and fearless, for He says, "And when these things begin to come to pass, then look up, and lift up your heads, for your redemption draweth nigh" (Luke 21:28).

The Persecuted Christ

Jesus Christ certainly understood the implications of His mission to redeem mankind, and that He would suffer and die on the Cross, as the Nicene Creed states. The Lord, Who "for us men and for our salvation, came down from heaven, and was incarnate of the Holy Spirit and the Virgin Mary, and became Man: and was crucified for us under Pontius Pilate, and suffered and was buried."

Though a painful, ignoble and unjust death awaited Him, the Lord did not live morosely, neither was He without hope and joy. "Enter into the joy of thy Lord," (Mat. 25:21) He tells His servants. Even on the night of His betrayal He says, "Peace I leave with you, my peace I give unto you" (John 14:27). If it be argued that Jesus

Christ, being the Son of God, surely possessed more inner resources of joy and peace than we, consider as well the martyrs of the Church, both from Apostolic to modern times. Throughout history untold numbers have endured privation, loss, torture and death rather than renounce their faith in God.

God-hating Caesars of Rome and the atheists of Soviet Communism foreshadow and presage the black reign of Antichrist. Yet the fathers teach that end times Christians will be blessed and rewarded above others for what they endure. St. Cyril of Jerusalem writes, "Who then is that blessed man, that shall at that time devoutly witness for Christ? For I say that the martyrs of that time excel all martyrs. For the martyrs hitherto have wrestled with men only; but in the time of Antichrist they shall do battle with Satan in his own person"[184]

The "hope and comfort" of avoiding persecutions, especially the greatest persecutions, is unworthy of a mankind created to take his place among the angels. Far better is that inner comfort of facing and enduring them with God's help.

Immanency Destroyed?

Modern premillennialists also object that their Rapture must be an unexpected event occurring prior to the tribulation, because anything else

---

[184] Cyril of Jerusalem, *Catechetical Lectures*, XV, 17.

destroys immanency, the very force that has produced so much dedication in times of persecution, worldly environment, and theological confusion. From the days of the apostle Paul until today, the Christian who was convinced his Lord could come at any moment was motivated to holy living, soul winning, and missionary zeal.[185]

Immanency according to premillennialism is the idea that Christ may return at any moment. LaHaye claims this is needed for Christians to be motivated. Frankly, that sounds like those employees who won't stay busy unless they think the boss might walk into their office unexpectedly. Why must Christ's return seem immanent for believers to be actively engaged in God's work? Does that possibility really change anything? God's Last Judgment must be faced in any case, and one's use or misuse of his or her talents accounted for. Besides, Christ is already immanent among Orthodox Christians, for they receive His Body and Blood in the sacrament of Communion. Beyond this, the Lord also promises, "I am with you always, even unto the end of the world" (Mat. 28:20).

Besides, each person faces a real immanency that is not subject to speculation, although it is definitely related to eschatology (the study of ultimate things), and that is his or her own death. This could happen at any time, and certainly will occur eventually. Yet in spite of this dramatic, impending fate and the subsequent pros-

---

[185] Tim LaHaye, *Rapture*, p. 112.

pect of meeting God face to face, not many practice living as though each day might be their last. And, as the Lord says, "If you be not able to do that thing which is least, why take ye thought for the rest?" (Luke 12:26).

But, as was pointed out earlier, Christ's return is perpetually immanent, for many people — probably the majority of mortals — won't be ready when it happens. Regarding this, premillennialists object that they are far too clever to be taken unawares. "The glorious appearing will not take Bible-taught Christians by surprise," says LaHaye, "for they will expect it exactly seven years after the signing of the covenant between Israel and the Antichrist."[186]

Similarly sure of themselves, Peter and Patti La-Londe have thoughtfully written an instruction book for those readers they expect to be "left behind" after the premillennialist rapture. Never mind that even the angels in heaven do not know when Jesus will return, and never mind that the Lord Himself warns, "in such an hour as ye think not the Son of man cometh" (Mat. 24:44) — the LaLondes have an inside track: "You know the exact date when Jesus will return to this earth to set up His kingdom just as He promised the prophet Daniel. All you have to do is take the date of the rapture and add seven biblical years."[187]

However, this over-confidence is a sure sign of trouble, and St. John Chrysostom explains how it is that

[186] Tim LaHaye, *Rapture*, p. 204.
[187] Peter & Patti LaLond, *Left Behind* (Eugene, OR: Harvest House Publishers, 1995), p. 95.

the very signs of the end times allow the evil day to come upon people unexpectedly.

> For travail, indeed, you say, does not come upon the pregnant woman unexpectedly: for she knows that after nine months the birth will take place. And yet it is very uncertain. For some bring forth at the seventh month, and others at the ninth. And at any rate the day and the hour is uncertain. With respect to this therefore, Paul speaks thus. And the image is exact. For there are not many sure signs of travail; many indeed have brought forth in the high roads, or when out of their houses and abroad, not fore-seeing it. And he has not only glanced here at the uncertainty, but also at the bitterness of the pain. For as she while sporting, laughing, not looking for anything at all, being suddenly seized with unspeakable pains, is pierced through with the pangs of labor—so will it be with those souls, when the Day comes upon them."[188]

Not Enough Time

Another peculiar argument premillennialists have mustered in defense of their rapture theory is that "there isn't enough time" for the "wedding of the Lamb" to take place. "Two very significant, time-

---

[188] John Chrysostom, *Homilies on the Gospel of Matthew*, IX.

consuming events await the church after the Rapture and before the Glorious Appearing," says LaHaye.

> At the Judgment Seat of Christ (Romans 14:10 and 2 Corinthians 5:10) every Christian will give account of himself to God for the deeds done in the flesh (described in detail in 1 Corinthians 3:9-15). According to 1 Corinthians 4:5, this Judgment Seat occurs after the Rapture. The Wedding and Marriage Supper of the Lamb (Revelations 19:7-9) follow the Judgment Seat, just prior to the Glorious Appearing. Only the pre-Trib position allows sufficient time (at least seven years) for such events to be fulfilled with dignity and grace. The post-Trib believer is forced to relegate both the Judgment Seat of Christ for millions of people and the Marriage Ceremony and Supper of the Lamb to "the twinkling of an eye" — or ignore them altogether.[189]

It is astonishing that pre-Trib writers fancy they know how much time God needs to achieve His ends. Why are seven years required for the consummation of the world when the Lord was able to create the entire universe in only six days? Especially since, according to patristic writers, the creative acts of each of those six days took place instantaneously. We meet eternity in this present moment, and St. John Chysostom points out that time as reckoned by humans already ceases to

---

[189] Tim LaHaye, *Rapture*, p. 202.

be operational at the Lord's Return: "Therefore he said not, 'after the tribulation,' but immediately 'after the tribulation of those days shall the sun be darkened,' for almost at the same time all things come to pass."[190]

Is it really to be supposed that our Omniscient God requires each soul to actually stand before Him and recite all past deeds? And that this examination will consume days, hours and minutes as humans calculate these intervals? Even many at death's door have related that their entire lives pass before their eyes—completely and comprehensibly—in an instant. Therefore we see again that the "need" for the Rapture to occur prior to the tribulation does not survive close scrutiny.

Beyond this, the Lord indicates that Christians are to be watching for His return from the wedding, and waiting for his beckoning knock. "Let your loins be girded about, and your lights burning; and ye yourselves like unto men that wait for their lord, when he will return from the wedding; that when he cometh and knocketh, they may open unto him immediately" (Luke 12:35-36). How does this accord with the premillennialist notion that Christians will already be raptured into heaven at that time?

Good and Bad Remain Until the Very End

Many Scriptural passages are force-fit to validate the modern rapture concept for the simple reason that it

---

[190] John Chrysostom, *Homilies on the Gospel According to St. Matthew*, LXXVI, 3.

has no sound theological or Biblical basis. The very idea of a pre-Trib rapture would never have been thought up, in fact, if it hadn't been for weaknesses in the premillennialist end-times scheme that needed mending. Hal Lindsey admits this deficiency in *The Late Great Planet Earth:*

> Here is the chief reason why we believe the Rapture occurs before the Tribulation: the prophets have said that God will set up a Kingdom on earth over which the Messiah will rule. There will be mortal people in that Kingdom. If the Rapture took place at the same time as the Second Coming, there would be no mortals left who would be believers; therefore, there would be no one to go into the Kingdom and repopulate the earth. We need to understand that during the seven-year Tribulation there will be people who will become believers at that time. In spite of persecution as described in the previous chapter, they will survive this terrible period of history and will be taken with Christ to reign with Him for 1000 years. This is the Kingdom which is God's prelude to eternity.[191]

Here we see the result of Irenaeus' conception of Christ's millennial reign fulfilled in Old Testament prophecy: another premillennialist notion that runs afoul the Scriptures. Lindsey proposes that God will separate believers from non-believers, the "good" from

---

[191] Hal Lindsey, *The Late Great Planet Earth,* p. 132.

the "bad," a full seven years before the Last Judgment. In contrast, the Bible and fathers of the Church clearly say otherwise. Consider, for example, the parable of the wheat and the tares (Mat. 13:24-30).

Here the Lord not only shows that the wheat and tares are together until the moment of harvest, but that in fact the tares are gathered *first*. And the reason that they are left together until the end is to allow every opportunity for the tares to have a change of heart and become wheat, as St. John Chrysostom points out,

> But what means, "Lest ye root up the wheat with them?" Either He means this, If ye are to take up arms, and to kill the heretics, many of the saints also must needs be overthrown with them; or that of the very tares it is likely that many may change and become wheat. If therefore ye root them up beforehand, ye injure that which is to become wheat, slaying some, in whom there is yet room for change and improvement.[192]

The Rapture as Ruse

Finally, what are the negative implications of belief in the Rapture? First, those who so believe are basing their convictions on the falseness of non-scriptural and non-patristic doctrine, which universally leads to further errors. Second, the misplaced hope of being absent

---

[192] John Chrysostom, *Homilies on the Gospel of Matthew*, XLVIII.

during the Great Tribulation renders one totally unprepared for Antichrist's actual advent. Consider the words of Protestant theologian Arthur Pink, who presumptuously declares, "The Antichrist cannot appear before the Rapture of the saints." As long as the rapture has not yet occurred, "then, here is proof positive that the Antichrist *has not yet appeared*."[193]

It is by no means far-fetched to conceive the premillennialist concept of rapture as one of Antichrist's methods for rendering what should be a particularly resistant segment of the population to be exceptionally vulnerable instead. Rather than being prepared to endure all for Christ's sake, premillennialists are convinced they will suffer nothing.[194]

The sudden acceptance of rapture indoctrination (books, movies, etc.) may in fact be a preemptive strike from the enemy—a demoralizing night attack intended to weaken opposition before the main troops actually appear. For how will the masses of people filled with premillennialist notions (those who confidently expect to abandon their cars "in case of rapture") react when that calamity they thought to avoid hits them head on? Will they feel betrayed? Led astray? Will they continue

[193] Arthur W. Pink, *The Antichrist,* p.33.
[194] We leave aside here the most fundamental question—which this author has never seen discussed in any dispensational literature—namely: if the premillennialist rapture were in fact true, what assurance would any particular premillennialists have of being included in it?

to trust those who led them down the rosy path to destruction? As Jim Bakker thoughtfully concedes,

> There is no biblical basis to believe in a pretribulational Rapture... Instead of the Church presenting a false hope by preaching the pretribulation Rapture, we should be spending this time informing believers that they will have to pass through the Tribulation, or at least some part of it. We should be teaching people to fall in love with Jesus. We should be spending our time, energy and resources getting spiritually ready for a severe period of persecution and a time of unparalleled upheaval."[195]

---

[195] Jim Bakker, *Prosperity and the Coming Apocalypse* (Nashville, TN: Thomas Nelson Pub., 1998), pp. 123, 125-126.

CHAPTER TEN

The Wrath of God

Hubert University was the scene of a strange incident in its early days. One of the freshman students was son of a poor country farmer who was determined that his boy should get the education he never had himself. After the lad had been in school for a semester the old man paid a visit to the dormitory to see how he was doing.

"Well son, what are they larnin' you?" he asked.

"All kinds of things, Pa," the boy answered excitedly as he leafed through a mathematics book. "Why, this here is teaching me how to calculate the area of circle. Listen!" He began to recite an equation, "πr^2 . . . " But the young student got no further than this, for his father stood up with a shout and rushed out of the room with dust flying. He marched to the administration office, stormed in, and angrily banged on the dean's door.

"Is something wrong, sir?" the dean asked as he opened upon the obviously irate figure.

"That's what I want to know," the old man shouted. "Is somethin' wrong with you highfalootin'smart folks? What kind of tom-foolishness are you teachin' my boy?"

"I'm sure we can clear this up if you'll just calm down and tell me what your son said," the dean consoled.

The father harrumphed, then replied, "He said pie are square!"

"Oh yes, well, all freshmen learn that," the dean answered with a smile.

"What?" the old man exclaimed. "Look here, Mister Edeecation. I'm checking my son out of this crazy place today."

"But why?" the dean asked helplessly.

"Because pie are *round* — *cornbread* are square!"

Unlike this country farmer, God has clear and rational reasons for His anger. The Scriptures say that God sent His son to help us believe, and is therefore angry with those who do not do so: "He that believeth on the Son hath everlasting life: and he that believeth not the Son shall not see life; but the wrath of God abideth on him" (John 3:36).

The Scriptures say that God, through His Son, revealed perfect obedience, love, and righteousness, and enabled men to imitate Him, and is angry with those who refuse to live virtuously: "For the wrath of God is revealed from heaven against all ungodliness and unrighteousness of men, who hold the truth in unrighteousness" (Rom. 1:18).

The Scriptures say that God, through His Son, revealed the Way, the Truth and the Life, that is, salvation, and is angry with those who refuse to repent and be saved: "After thy hardness and impenitent heart treasurest up unto thyself wrath against the day of wrath and revelation of the righteous judgment of God" (Rom. 2:5).

The Scriptures say that God hates sin and is angry with those who prefer to be separated from Him: "Fornication, uncleanness, inordinate affection, evil concupiscence, and covetousness, which is idolatry: for which sake the wrath of God cometh upon the children of disobedience" (Col. 3:6).

The Scriptures say that God is angry with those who do not love Him—for these are His enemies: "The Lord will take vengeance on his adversaries, and he reserveth wrath for his enemies" (Na. 1:2).

Christians, those who keep God's commandments, are not subject to God's wrath, as St. Paul says, "Much more then, being now justified by his blood, we shall be saved from wrath through him" (Rom. 5:9).

God's Wrath Equals the Great Tribulation?

The question then is not whether Christians should expect to endure God's wrath, for it is manifest that He is angry with others. Rather, the question is, what *is* God's wrath, and can it reasonably be interpreted as the Great Tribulation?

The following verse is often cited by premillennialists as proof that God's wrath is synonymous with the Great Tribulation: "And the third angel followed them, saying with a loud voice, if any man worship the beast and his image, and receive his mark in his forehead or in his hand, the same shall drink of the wine of the wrath of God" (Rev. 14:9). According to LaHaye, this place in Revelations is inarguably "during the wrath portion in chapters 6-18."[196] In fact, it is close to the end of that part of the text. Yet, how can this "wine of the wrath of God" be the same thing *as* the Great Tribulation, if it is only poured out somewhere *during* and even *near the end* of the Great Tribulation?

Another verse favored as evidence of the same assertion is: "For God hath not appointed us to wrath, but to obtain salvation by our Lord Jesus Christ"(1 Thes. 5:9). Ironically, the verse contains within itself the elements of undoing the premillennialist position. The meaning of "wrath" can be deduced by considering the word to which St. Paul opposed it, namely, "salvation." As salvation is an eternal condition, we may presume that God's wrath against His enemies shall be eternal as well. The Great Tribulation will no doubt be terrible, but it is nevertheless prophesied to last but a short time. It is reasonable to understand God's wrath as not being this passing circumstance, but the experience of eternity in hell for damned souls.

"Thus God has not inclined to this that He might destroy us, but that He might save us," says St. John Chrysostom about this same verse.

> And whence is it manifest that this is His will? He has given His own Son for us. So does He desire that we should be saved, that He has given His Son, and not merely given, but given Him to death. From these considerations hope is produced. For do not despair of thyself, O

[196] Tim LaHaye, *Rapture*, p. 203.

man, in going to God, who has not spared even His Son for thee. Faint not at present evils. He who gave His Only-Begotten, that He might save thee and deliver thee from hell, what will He spare henceforth for thy salvation? So that thou oughtest to hope for all things kind. For neither should we fear, if we were going to a judge who was about to judge us, and who had shown so much love for us, as to have sacrificed his son. Let us hope therefore for kind and great things, for we have received the principal thing; let us believe, for we have seen an example; let us love, for it is the extreme of madness for one not to love who has been so treated.[197]

The Hour of Temptation

One of the arguments for pre-Trib rapture is that God's wrath is intended not for Christians. With this point alone, the Orthodox can agree, as the above verses indicate. Yet premillennialists allege that by God's "wrath" is to be understood nothing other than the Great Tribulation. And this, of course, they feel entitled to avoid. "The hope and comfort of the Rapture," says LaHaye, "demands that we escape the Tribulation, being raptured out of this world before God's wrath begins."[198]

[197] John Chrysostom, *Homilies on Thessalonians*, V, 9.
[198] Tim LaHaye, *Rapture*, p. 68.

Another verse cited in this line of thinking comes from Revelations, where the Lord promises to keep Christians from the hour of temptation. "Because thou hast kept the word of my patience, I also will keep thee from the hour of temptation, which shall come upon all the world, to try them that dwell upon the earth" (Rev. 3:10). This "hour of temptation" may well refer to the period of last days tribulation. If so, the "hour" suggests the brevity of the period, which Jesus elsewhere said would be shortened for the elect's sake.

Premillennialists assert that God will keep Christians from the hour of temptation by taking them altogether out of the world (the Rapture). Yet, other Scriptures do not support such a conclusion. Our Lord Himself prayed to God the Father thus: "I pray not that thou shouldest take them out of the world, but that thou shouldest keep them from the evil" (John 17:15).

The Old Testament is replete with accounts of those whom God allowed to undergo trial and temptation. Consider Shadrach, Meshach and Abednego, who were threatened with a furnace heated seven times hotter than usual because they would not worship King Nebuchadnezzar. Their story is a metaphor for the end times, for they were not wisked out of danger by some kind of spiritual safety net. Yet, Nebuchadnezzar said, "Lo, I see four men loose, walking in the midst of the fire, and they have no hurt; and the form of the fourth is like a son of the gods" (Dan. 3:24-25).

The Lord is able to preserve those He loves by means of His presence. This alone is enough to calm storms and feed multitudes. And shall not He whose word is "sharper than any two-edged sword, piercing even to the dividing asunder of soul and spirit" (Heb. 4:12) distinguish and separate those in His protection from those who are not? Let us recall how that Israel was in bondage to Egypt, and the Lord sent plagues to compel Pharaoh to acknowledge His power and to let His children go (Ex. 11:4-7).

The Israelites, God's chosen people, were very much present in Egypt during these plagues that destroyed Egypt's hope, but God protected them. Every first born of the Egyptians died, from man to beast, but not an Israelite was touched. God is able to distinguish between those He protects and those He chastens. We should by no means fear that we might live during the Great Tribulation; we should only fear that we may not be in God's presence.

Archbishop Averky points out that these Egyptian plagues were signs of the destruction by God that shall happen in the last days: "The symbol of these plagues is taken from the plagues which struck ancient Egypt, whose defeat was a prefiguration of the defeat of the false Christian kingdom which above has been called Egypt, and then Babylon."[199]

The Tribulation is for Sinners

Based on his premillennial stance, namely that because of the rapture no Christians will be on earth during the tribulation, LaHaye asserts that "the Tribu-

---

[199] Archbishop Averky Taushev, p. 215.

lation... is not intended for the church! It is meant for Israel and the Gentile."[200]

The Protestant penchant for materializing spiritual themes has already been noted, and the effect of this in modern rapture theory is to convert spiritual transformation at the Lord's Second Coming into some kind of cosmic amusement park ride. Yet there is validity in the idea that the Tribulation, and everything else concerned with the last days, will primarily affect non-Christians. This does not mean that Christians will be physically absent, but rather that they will not be influenced in the same way as non-Christians.

Those who are resurrected in the first resurrection, who are participants in the sacramental life of the Church through the Holy Spirit, have already in this world begun to abide in heaven. These have entered Paradise, though Tribulation may be all around them. Metropolitan Hierotheos writes:

> St. Simeon [the New Theologian] makes an extensive analysis saying that the Second Coming of Christ and the judgment to come will be chiefly for the sinners, who are living in passions and sin, but not for the saints, who are already experiencing the Paradise of Christ. As many as are children of that light and are sons of the coming day, "on them the day of the Lord will never come." When the Christian in fear and trembling keeps the commandments of Christ and lives in repentance, he becomes

[200] Tim LaHaye, *Rapture,* p. 65.

218

united with that light, and so in reality in this life he passes through the judgment. The judgment takes place essentially in this life. The person who sees the light is baptized with the Holy Spirit and does not take into account the day of the Lord. So in this way the Second Coming will appear mainly to the sinners, who have lived with passions during their present life and not kept the commandments of God. For the saint it is a natural state, which they are experiencing now.[201]

St. Simeon the New Theologian declares that the day of the Lord may seem to such Christians no different than another day, since to them Christ has already come:

Such a man is not judged by the judgment and justice to come, for he has been judged beforehand, and he is not censured by that light, for he has been enlightened beforehand, nor is he tested or burned on entering that fire, for he has been tested beforehand. It is not then, in his opinion, that the day of the Lord appears, for it has become altogether one bright and shining day, thanks to the conversation and company of God.[202]

[201] Metropolitan Hierotheos (Vlachos), *Life After Death*, pp. 211-212.
[202] Simeon the New Theologian, *Ethical Treatise*, 10, *SC* 129, p. 266.

CHAPTER ELEVEN

Where the Church Is Not

Holy Scriptures and fathers of the Church teach that when the strong man is released — when the dragon is loosed — he will be angry, knowing that his time is short. "Woe to the inhabiters of the earth and the sea! For the devil is come down unto you, having great wrath, because he knoweth that he hath but a short time" (Rev. 12:12).

The Prophet Daniel speaks of a week of seven days, by which we understand this period of suffering to last seven years. This seven-year period is divided into two halves, with the second half expected to be what is called the Great Tribulation. This time of the dragon's release from bondage is also supposed to correspond with the advent of Antichrist upon the world stage.

The Scriptures and patristic writers offer considerable detail regarding what Antichrist will be and do, such that his advent and identity as a villain ought to be apparent to all. But such will not be the case. He who is led by the father of lies will easily seduce the masses. The Bible warns that, were it not for God's protection he would "deceive the very elect" (Mat. 24:24).

When mankind has been prepared to receive Antichrist unconditionally, then he will appear. And this process of preparation is well underway, as with each passing year there exists a growing willingness among people to accept as normal and good what before was considered abnormal and bad. St. John describes the scene in which Antichrist enslaves those already darkened by worldliness and sends them as his pawns out to destroy the Church:

> And when the thousand years are expired, Satan shall be loosed from his prison, And shall go out to deceive the nations which are in the four quarters of the earth, Gog and Magog, to gather them together to battle: the number of whom is as the sand of the sea. And they went up on the breadth of the earth, and compassed the camp of the saints about (Rev. 20: 7-9).

These are the stooges Antichrist will manipulate in his quest to exterminate Christianity. Gog and Magog encompass not merely the saints, but the *camp* of the saints, meaning the Church. Augustine says,

> This then is his purpose in seducing them, to draw them to this battle. For even before this he was wont to use as many and various seductions as he could continue. And the words 'he shall go out' mean, he shall burst forth from lurking hatred into open persecution. For this persecution, occurring while the final judgment is imminent, shall be the last which shall be endured by the holy Church throughout the world, the whole city of Christ being assailed

by the whole city of the devil, as each exists on earth.[203]

There has been considerable speculation about the meanings of the words Gog and Magog. Some writers have traced them back to particular tribes of peoples, and put forth the theory that these peoples, in their modern descendants, will be at Antichrist's beck and call. Augustine takes a much broader view, saying these names represent that portion of humanity in general which by its darkened nature allowed Satan to be shut up in the evil within it. This again is reminiscent of the "house" of Satan, which Christ despoiled:

> For these nations which he calls names and Magog are not to be understood as some barbarous nations in some part of the world, or some other foreign nations not under Roman government. For John marks that they are spread over the whole earth, when he says, "the nations which are in the four corners of the earth," and he added that these are God and Magog. The meaning of these names we find to be Gog, "a roof," Magog, "from a roof" — a house, as it were, and he who comes out of the house. They are therefore the nations in which the devil was shut up as in an abyss, and the devil himself coming out from them and going forth, so that they are the roof, he from the roof.[204]

---

[203] Augustine, *City of God*, XX, 11.
[204] Augustine, *City of God*, XX, 11.

The Gates of Hell

If ever a time in history could be characterized as one in which the "gates of hell" were to be opened on earth, the period of the Great Tribulation must certainly be it. Perhaps this is what the Lord meant when He said, "When ye shall see all these things, know that it is near, even at the doors" (Mat. 24:33). Yet Christians need not fear, for "I will build my church, and the gates of hell shall not prevail against it" (Mat. 16:18).

From Christ Himself we learn that even in the darkest hours of Antichrist's reign, the Church will exist on earth. "There shall be a Church in this world even when the devil shall be loosed, as there has been since the beginning, and shall be always," says St. Augustine.

> "And they went up on the breadth of the earth, and compassed the camp of the saints about." This relates to the last judgment, but I have thought fit to mention it now, lest any one might suppose that in that short time during which the devil shall be loose there shall be no Church upon earth, whether because the devil finds no Church, or destroys it by manifold persecutions.[205]

The Woman Clothed with the Sun

The strong man, then, is loosed from the house in which he was bound at the Lord's first coming. He is

---

[205] Augustine, *City of God*, XX, 8.

angry with his past bondage, and especially angry with Him who did the binding, and she who was allowed to flourish during that time. This she, of course, is the Holy Church, the woman mentioned in Revelation against whom the dragon is angry:

> And there appeared a great wonder in heaven—a woman clothed with the sun, and the moon under her feet, and upon her head a crown of twelve stars. And she, being with child, cried, travailing in birth, and pained to be delivered. And the dragon stood before the woman which was ready to be delivered, for to devour her child as soon as it was born (Rev. 12:1-3).

Premillennialists think this woman represents Israel, based on the persecutions Jews have endured for most of their history. Hal Lindsey says,

> I don't believe it's mere coincidence that the first prophetic reference to a woman who will bear a child is found in the *first* book of the Bible, and the last reference to a pregnant woman is found in the *last* book of the Bible, and in *both cases* the child is to crush Satan. It seems likely to me that the woman and child in both of these passages are referring to Israel and her offspring, the Messiah Jesus.[206]

---

[206] Hal Lindsey, *There's a New World Coming*, p. 160.

Yet, such arbitrary speculation is not supported by Scripture. Far from being a brilliant wife bringing forth a favored child, Israel was portrayed as faithless and divorced when God, through the prophets, said, "for all the causes whereby backsliding Israel committed adultery I had put her away" (Jer. 3:8).

Besides, why should the dragon bother persecuting a nation and people that after two thousand years still hasn't recognized its own Messiah? Satan may very well exploit and manipulate the self-centeredness of the Jews—even as he manipulated the Pharisees to call for the crucifixion of their Anointed One. But his hatred is toward the Church, toward Christians, for these are they "which keep the commandments of God, and have the testimony of Jesus Christ."

As usual, premillennialists remain apart with their private opinions, rather than trusting in the wisdom of the Church as transmitted through the fathers, which are unanimous as to the woman's identity: "The woman clothed with the sun," writes Victorinus, "and having the moon under her feet, and wearing a crown of twelve stars upon her head, and travailing in her pains, is the ancient Church of fathers, and prophets, and saints, and apostles."[207]

The question is sometimes raised whether this woman might represent the Virgin Mary. To this, Archbishop Averky replies,

---

[207] Victorinus, *Commentary on the Apocalypse of the Blessed John,* XII, 1.

Such outstanding commentators as St. Hippolytus, St. Methodius, and St. Andrew of Caesarea find this is "the Church clothed with the Word of the Father, shining more brightly than the sun." From the fact that she is in pain during childbirth, it is evident that it is incorrect to see in this woman the Most Holy Theotokos, for the giving birth from Her of the Son of God was without pain. These torments of birth-giving signify the difficulties which had to be overcome by the Church of Christ when it was being established in the world (martyrdom, the spreading of heresies).[208]

The Church continually brings forth Jesus Christ into the world, even as He first brought the Church into the world: "By the 'woman then clothed with the sun,' he meant most manifestly the Church, endued with the Father's word, whose brightness is above the sun," says Hippolytus.

And by the "moon under her feet" he referred to her being adorned, like the moon, with heavenly glory. And the words, "upon her head a crown of twelve stars," refer to the twelve apostles by whom the Church was founded. And those, "she, being with child, cries, travailing in birth, and pained to be delivered," mean that the Church will not cease to bear from her heart the Word that is persecuted by

[208]Archbishop Averky Taushev, p. 178.

the unbelieving in the world. "And she brought forth," he says, 'a man-child, who is to rule all the nations;' by which is meant that the Church, always bringing forth Christ, the perfect man-child of God, who is declared to be God and man, becomes the instructor of all the nations.[209]

Wroth with the Woman

Certain aspects of Genesis are mirrored in the Book of Revelation, suggesting our Lord's saying, "the last shall be first, and the first last" (Mat. 20:9). For instance, in the first days a serpent tempted the woman Eve, and through her brought about the demise of humanity. In the last days, a dragon is to tempt the woman clothed with the sun, yet without success.

This woman, the Church, resists the dragon's temptations and evil charms. More, she produces seed that—unlike the serpent—keep the commandments of God. Because of this, the dragon hates the woman and wants to destroy all her progeny: "And the dragon was wroth with the woman, and went to make war with the remnant of her seed, which keep the commandments of God, and have the testimony of Jesus Christ" (Rev. 12:13-14).

St. Augustine exclaims, "He who reads this passage, even half asleep, cannot fail to see that the kingdom of Antichrist shall fiercely, though for a short

[209] Hippolytus, *The Works of Hippolytus*, II, 61.

time, assail the Church before the last judgment of God shall introduce the eternal reign of the saints."[210]

Wings of an Eagle

The woman clothed with the sun is preserved from the dragon by means of flight: "And to the woman were given two wings of a great eagle, that she might fly into the wilderness, into her place, where she is nourished for a time and times, and half a time, from the face of the serpent" (Rev. 12:14). There are various interpretations for the meaning of these wings, and they may in fact represent more than one thing. Archbishop Averky sees in them the Old and New Testaments.[211]

Victorinus believes the wings represent those two great prophets, Elias and Enoch, who were taken up alive into heaven and are to appear again in the last days: "'Two great wings' are the two prophets—Elias, and the prophet who shall be with him."[212]

Hippolytus finds in these wings faith in Jesus Christ:

> The Church [is] possessed of no other defense than the two wings of the great eagle, that is to say, the faith of Jesus Christ, who, in stretching forth His holy hands on the holy tree, unfolded two wings, the right and the left, and called to

[210] Augustine, *City of God*, XX, 23.

[211] Archbishop Averky Taushev, p. 184.

[212] Victorinus, *Commentary on the Apocalypse of the Blessed John*, XII, 13.

Him all who believed upon Him, and covered them as a hen her chickens. For by the mouth of Malachi also He speaks thus: "And unto you that fear my name shall the Sun of righteousness arise with healing in His wings."[213]

By contrast, Protestant writer Hal Lindsey offers an earthbound interpretation of the passage. He suggests the wings represent no spiritual reality, but rather a military airplane: "Some kind of a massive airlift will rapidly transport these fleeing Jews across rugged terrain to their place of protection. Since the eagle is the national symbol of the United States, it's possible that the airlift will be made available by aircraft from the U.S Sixth Fleet in the Mediterranean."[214]

The Church in Flight

Time and times and half a time add up to three and a half times, representing three and one half years, or the second half of Daniel's week of seven years. This is considered to be the worst time which humanity will ever endure. Jesus called it the Great Tribulation, and it is in these years that Antichrist is expected to show his brutal and utterly evil visage to the world. Hippolytus says, "That refers to the one thousand two hundred and threescore days (the half of the week) during which the tyrant is to reign and persecute the Church, which flees

---

[213] Hippolytus, *The Works of Hippolytus,* II, 61.
[214] Hal Lindsey, *There's a New World Coming,* p. 165.

from city to city, and seeks concealment in the wilderness among the mountains."[215]

According to the Lord's own direction, Christians are permitted, even encouraged, to seek sanctuary in hiding during these difficult times. "The Lord, knowing the greatness of the adversary, grants indulgence to the godly, saying, Then let them which be in Judaea flee to the mountains," says St. Cyril of Jerusalem.

> But if any man is conscious that he is very stout-hearted, to encounter Satan, let him stand (for I do not despair of the Church's nerves), and let him say, who shall separate us from the love of Christ and the rest? But, let those of us who are fearful provide for our own safety; and those who are of a good courage, stand fast: for then shall be great tribulation, such as hath not been from the beginning of the world until now, no, nor ever shall be. But thanks be to God who hath confined the greatness of that tribulation to a few days; for He says, but for the elect's sake those days shall be shortened; and Antichrist shall reign for three years and a half only. For this cause we must hide ourselves and flee.[216]

On this point there is great unanimity among patristic writers—Christians should take whatever measures they can to distance themselves from the

---

[215] Hippolytus, *The Works of Hippolytus,* II, 61.
[216] Cyril of Jerusalem, *Catechetical Lectures,* XV, 16.

great evil of Antichrist. According to St. Andrew of Caesarea, "So it is always, but especially at the coming of Antichrist who will reign for three and one-half years. At that time it may be there will escape from him those who have hidden in the literal wilderness—the mountains, holes, and caves."[217]

Lactantius suggests that the general devastation of earth (and society, no doubt) will be the signal to run: "Thus the earth shall be laid waste, as though by one common robbery. When these things shall so happen, then the righteous and the followers of truth shall separate themselves from the wicked, and flee into solitudes."[218]

Hippolytus encourages us with the thought that Antichrist's three and one half years will pass quickly, even for those hiding in caves:

> Not even then will the merciful and benignant God leave the race of men without all comfort; but He will shorten even those days and the period of three years and a half, and He will curtail those times on account of the remnant of those who hide themselves in the mountains and caves, that the phalanx of all those saints fail not utterly. But these days shall run their course rapidly; and the kingdom of the deceiver and Antichrist shall be speedily removed."[219]

---

[217] Andrew of Caesarea, *Commentary on the Apocalypse*, XXXV.
[218] Lactantius, *Divine Institutes*, XVII.
[219] Hippolytus, *Appendix to the Works of Hippolytus*, XXXV.

St. John Chrysostom also reflects that this brief period is for the benefit of believers: "But whom doth He here mean by the elect? The believers that were shut up in the midst of them. For if the Jewish war was shortened for the elect's sake, much more shall this temptation be limited for these same's sake"[220]

Even the Old Testament indicates that the faithful will hide for a short time, corresponding to that relatively brief period in which Antichrist (clearly indicated by the words "serpent" and "dragon") is to hold power:

> Come my people, enter into thy chambers, and shut thy doors about thee: hide thyself as it were for a little moment, until the indignation be overpast. For, behold, the Lord cometh out of his place to punish the inhabitants of the earth for their iniquity: the earth also shall disclose her blood, and shall no more cover her slain. In that day the Lord with his sore and great and strong sword shall punish leviathan the piercing serpent, even leviathan that crooked serpent; and he shall slay the dragon that is in the sea (Is. 26:20-27:1).

How is it that the faithful will be preserved? Hippolytus adds this:

> But many who are hearers of the divine Scriptures, and have them in their hand, and keep them in mind with understanding, will escape

[220] John Chysostom, *Homilies According to the Gospel of St. Matthew,* LXXVI, 2.

his [Antichrist's] imposture. For they will see clearly through his insidious appearance and his deceitful imposture, and will flee from his hands, and betake themselves to the mountains, and hide themselves in the caves of the earth; and they will seek after the Friend of man with tears and a contrite heart; and He will deliver them out of his toils, and with His right hand He will save those from his snares who in a worthy and righteous manner make their supplication to Him.[221]

The Lord again directs us to expect no permanent home during those times: "But when they persecute you in this city, flee ye into another: for verily I say unto you, Ye shall not have gone over the cities of Israel, till the Son of man be come" (Mat. 10:24).

No Church on Earth?

As we have already seen, premillennialist doctrine supposes that individual Christians will be "raptured" to heaven before the Great Tribulation begins. Believers shouldn't expect to be present during the end times simply because "Christians don't need that test," or so LaHaye sweepingly declares. "They have already made their decision for Christ and against Antichrist. Only lost souls will proceed into the Tribulation."[222]

---

[221] Hippolytus, *Appendix to the Works of Hippolytus*, XXXII.
[222] Tim LaHaye, *Rapture*, p.65, 66.

But it projects beyond even this an assumption that the Church itself will vanish from the earth. The Scriptural justification for these broad assertions reputedly comes from the absence of the word "church" in the middle chapters of the Book of Revelation.

Not only is Scripture totally silent about the church during the Gentile Tribulation period, but she appears immediately in [Revelation] chapter 19 at its end, already in heaven, coming down with Christ "with power and great glory."[223]

Premillennialists consider this to be proof that the Church—will have been raptured into heaven before the Great Tribulation: "In the first three chapters of Revelation the Church is mentioned nineteen times as being on earth," says Jeffrey. "However, from Revelation chapters 4 to 19, which begins to describe in great detail the Great Tribulation, there is not one mention of the Church on the earth."[224]

The Temple of God

Patristic writers, however, have found references to the Church exactly where the premillennialists say there are none. For instance, St. John writes,

And there was given me a reed like unto a rod: and the angel stood, saying, Rise, and measure

---

[223] Tim LaHaye, *Rapture*, p.65
[224] Grant R. Jeffrey, p. 135.

the temple of God, and the altar, and them that worship therein. But the court which is without the temple leave out, and measure it not; for it is given unto the Gentiles; and the holy city shall they tread under food forty and two months (Rev. 11:1-2).

What is the temple of God? It has various meanings, and all of them indicate the place where God is worshiped. From about the time of Moses until 70 A.D., the temple was a physical structure that housed the Holy of Holies and the Ark of the Covenant, and in which the Jews made their sacrifices to God.

But the temple is also spiritual. It is the place in heaven where God abides, for in the Psalms we read, "In my distress I called upon my Lord, and cried unto my God: he heard my voice out of his temple" (Psalm 18:6).

The temple is even a human body—the body of Jesus Christ—for He said, "Destroy this temple, and in three days I will raise it up" (John 2:19).

And after Christ's resurrection, the temple came to mean the Holy Church, as St. Paul points out:

Now therefore ye are no more strangers and foreigners, but fellow citizens with the saints, and of the household of God; and are built upon the foundation of the apostles and prophets, Jesus Christ himself being the chief corner stone; in whom all the building fitly framed together grows into an *holy temple in the Lord* (Eph. 2:19-21).

235

In speaking to the Church in Corinth, St. Paul wrote, "Know you not that ye are the temple of God, and that the Spirit of God dwells in you?" (1 Cor. 3:16). Consider also the Lord's words unto the Church of Philadelphia, found in that part of Revelations in which premillennialists agree that the church is plainly indicated: "Him that overcomes will I make a pillar in the *temple of my God*" (Rev. 3:10).

On the other hand, there is no passage in Scripture suggesting that "temple of God" is synonymous with Israel or the Jews. Therefore we are more than justified in assuming that the Church is indicated. Regarding this passage, St. Andrew of Caesarea affirms, "The temple of the living God is the Church in which the rational sacrifices are offered."[225]

And yet there is more in the passage to validate our point, according to Archbishop Averky. For the reference to forty-two months and the outer court specifically indicate that the Church on earth is to be present during the Great Tribulation.

> The treading of the Holy City, Jerusalem, or the ecumenical Church for the course of forty-two months signifies that at the coming of Antichrist the faithful will be persecuted for the course of three and a half years... The inner court which was measured signifies the "church of the firstborn in heaven" (cf. Heb. 12:23), the heavenly sanctuary; and that the outer court left without measurement is the

[225] Andrew of Caesarea, *Commentary on the Apocalypse*, 30.

Church of Christ on earth which must endure persecution at first from pagans and then, in the last times, from Antichrist. The miserable condition of the earthly Church is limited, however, to this period of forty-two months. The persecution touches only the outward court; that is, the outer side of the life of Christians whose property will be taken away. They will be subjected to tortures, while the inner sanctuary of their souls will remain untouched.[226]

Out of the Midst

Tim LaHaye quotes Victorinus' excellent *Commentary on the Apocalypse of the Blessed John* as supposedly supporting the premillennialist position:

As early as 270 A.D., St. Victorinus, Bishop of Petrau, wrote a commentary on the Book of Revelation in which he said, "And I saw another great and wonderful sign, seven angels having the seven last plagues; for in them is completed the indignation of God. For the wrath of God always strikes the obstinate people with seven plagues, that is, perfectly, as it is said in Leviticus; and these shall be in the last time, when the church shall have gone out of the midst." So it is clear that the teaching of the

---

[226] Archbishop Averky Taushev, p. 165-166.

church being taken out "in the last time,"
meaning the coming of Christ, was known as
early as the third century.[227]

Unfortunately for his argument, LaHaye misunder-
stands and misrepresents—unintentionally, we hope—
the saint. It can easily be shown that Victorinus firmly
believed the Church would be present on earth during
the Great Tribulation. In the same text to which LaHaye
refers, the saint writes,

> The little season signifies three years and six
> months, in which with all his power the devil
> will avenge himself through Antichrist against
> the Church... the devil shall be loosed, and will
> seduce the nations in the whole world, and will
> entice war against the Church, the number of
> whose foes will be as the sand of the sea.[228]

What Victorinus may have actually meant by his
words, "the church shall have gone out of the midst,"
accords with an earlier point in this chapter. If midst is
conceived as being a focus of human activity and attention, then the Church will have gone out of this because
of its members fleeing and hiding from Antichrist.

We may also consider the meaning of midst as St.
John the Theologian used it. Since Victorinus' *Commen-
tary on the Apocalypse of the Blessed John* is based on the
Book of Revelation, it may be he intended to use the

---

[227] Tim LaHaye, *Rapture,* p. 170.
[228] Victorinus, *Commentary of the Apocalypse of the Blessed John,*
XX, 1-3.

word similarly. "Midst" appears eleven times in Revelation, and in each instance it is used to suggest the kingdom of heaven: "He that hath an ear, let him hear what the Spirit saith unto the churches. To him that overcometh will I give to eat of the tree of life, which is in the midst of the paradise of God" (Rev. 2:7).

In these verses we read of the midst of the paradise of God, the midst of the throne, the midst of the elders, the midst of heaven, and the midst of the street proceeding out of the throne of God. In the context of the Book of Revelations at least, midst indicates nearness to God. Accordingly, Victorinus' comment might well be understood to mean that the Church of the last days "goes out" (in a sense) from the nearness of God in order to endure Satan's temptations.

God is under no obligation to release Satan from bondage during these times, but He does so in order to prove and refine Christians. Job serves as our example here; though a righteous man of unparalleled integrity, Satan was allowed to tempt him to the limit of human endurance, both to glorify Job by overcoming and to humiliate the devil. Our Lord Himself is another example, for he was delivered into the hands of sinful men, persecuted and put to death on the cross. And as He hung on the Cross, He cried out, "My God, my God, why hast thou forsaken me?"

When the seventh angel pours out his vial, a great earthquake breaks Babylon into three parts and causes the cities of the nations to fall. Huge hailstones fall out of heaven, against which the people of earth blaspheme. In the midst of this, St. John says, "And every island fled away, and the mountains were not found" (Rev. 16:20). This can indicate that the plagues of the seventh vial were kept from the islands and mountains, since these represent the refuges of God's people. Irenaeus says,

> the Churches... the Spirit terms "the islands" because they are established in the midst of turbulence, suffer the storm of blasphemies, exist as a harbor of safety to those in peril, and are a refuge to those who love the height of heaven."[229]

Victorinus offers a similar interpretation, saying, "Mountains and islands removed from their places intimate that in the last persecution . . . the good will be removed, seeking to avoid persecution."[230]

As It Was in Noah's Days

Consider Noah, who obeyed God and built an ark to preserve his family from the destruction that was to come. He worked on it a long time, no doubt rubbing shoulders with people destined to die in the flood. And when everything was ready, at God's chosen time, the clouds darkened. The same rain fell on both Noah and those outside—but God's Ark—a symbol of the Holy Church, protected him. "As it was in the days of Noah,

---

[229] Irenaeus, *Against Heresies*, 5:34:3.
[230] Victorinus, *Commentary on the Apocalypse of the Blessed John*, VI, 14.

so shall it be also in the days of the Son of man..." (Luke 17: 26-27).

Throughout sacred history we see examples in which God preserves His own people not by utterly removing them from danger, but by uniquely preserving them from it. It is as though He desires a witness to those who are punished, a sign that their evil fate is not arbitrary but deliberate, not accidental but chosen from on high, and that they may understand certain men and women are preserved from the torment through faith in God. Jim Bakker, a former premillennialist who saw the light, says,

> During these persecutions God did not magically remove His people from their tormentors' grasp, but gave them the grace necessary to go *through* their tortures. What makes us think God should cut us a break and allow us to escape before the onslaught of hell comes on the earth? Have we been more faithful than those early saints? Are we more worthy of an easy ride to heaven than they were?[231]

The story of Joseph, like that of Noah, prefigures the end times. When Joseph was elevated to a position of authority, Egypt experienced seven years of plenty followed by seven years of drought. Joseph went through the drought along with all others in Egypt at that time, yet his prudence and preparation enabled not only him but also those in his charge to survive the dif-

---

[231] Jim Bakker, p. 126.

ficulties. It is possible that those seven years of drought symbolize the seven years of Antichrist's reign. "For a hundred years while the ark was building, and the wood was being wrought, and the righteous man was calling aloud, there was no one who believed," says John Chrysostom.

> But because they did not believe the threat in words, they suffered the punishment in very deed. And this will be our fate too, if we shall not have believed. On this account it is that He compares His coming with the days of Noah, because as some disbelieved in that deluge, so will they in the deluge of hell. Were these things a threat? Were they not a fact? Then will not He, who then brought punishment upon them so suddenly, much more inflict it now also?[232]

Suffering Christianity

Suffering of any kind is the last thing worldly people want. They especially dislike pain of heart, which we normally call grief or mourning. For them, these words of the Lord seem incomprehensible: "Blessed are they that mourn; for they shall be comforted" (Mat. 5:4).

Yet, suffering is natural to Christianity, being a common experience of the human soul as it discerns its separation from a loving God. Man in his fallen state is

---

[232] John Chrysostom, *On Paul to the Thessalonians*, VIII.

wounded and sick. He cannot truly be happy or joyful until the healing of Christ begins. Were he never to mourn this broken condition, he would ever remain in it — and distant from his salvation.

For some, "pain of heart" occurs spontaneously as they penitentially approach Christ and perceive that He is already and always nearer than hands and feet. This suffering is sweet, though difficult to bear. Of it, St. Makarius writes, "God's wrath visits all who refuse the bitter cross of agony, the cross of active suffering."[233]

Historically, of course, Christians have also borne outward persecutions for their faith:

> We ourselves glory in you in the churches of God for your patience and faith in all your persecutions and tribulations that ye endure. Which is a manifest token of righteous judgment of God, that ye may be counted worthy of the kingdom of God, for which ye also suffer (2 Thes. 1:4-5).

"If they have persecuted me they will persecute you also," says the Lord. Nor is this suffering limited to occasional political epochs in which Christians may find themselves in the hands of atheistic or pagan government, since Christian suffering is an outward manifestation of inner love. Therefore we who desire to be with Christ and to abide in the kingdom of heaven are also destined to suffer, as St. Paul taught: "We must

[233] Quoted in Ware, *The Orthodox Way*, p. 130.

through much tribulation enter into the kingdom of God" (Acts 14:22).

According to the fathers, these difficulties and persecutions, far from being horrible events to be avoided, are for our benefit. St. Cyril of Jerusalem says,

> As in the persecutions which happen from time to time, God will permit these things, not because he wants power to hinder them, but because according to His wont He will through patience crown His champions like as He did His prophets and apostles; to the end that, having toiled for a little while they may inherit the eternal kingdom of heaven.[234]

That which is eternal in each of us will not be harmed by troubles, rather it will be set free from the bondage of human weakness and limitation. "For as the gold is tested by the fire and is made useful, so ye also are being tested in yourselves. Ye then that abide and pass through the fire will be purified by it. For as the old loses its dross, so ye also shall cast away all sorrow and tribulation, and shall be purified, and shall be useful," says *The Shepherd of Hermas*.[235]

Irenaeus sees in man a microcosm of the tares and wheat parable. Each person has within both that which of the devil, and that which is of God. These, he says, must be "broken up" and separated by tribulation, that

---

[234] Cyril of Jerusalem, *Catechetical Lectures*, XV, 17.
[235] *The Shepherd of Hermas*, I, II, III.

the chaff may be discarded leaving only the fine flour to serve at the Lord's feast:

> And therefore throughout all time, man, having been molded at the beginning by the hands of God, that is, of the Son and of the Spirit, is made after the image and likeness of God: the chaff, indeed, which is the apostasy, being cast away; but the wheat, that is, those who bring forth fruit to God in faith, being gathered into the barn. And for this cause tribulation is necessary for those who are saved, that having been after a manner broken up, and rendered fine, and sprinkled over by the patience of the Word of God, and set on fire [for purification], they may be fitted for the royal banquet.[236]

End Times Victors

Jesus leaves no doubt that His followers will be rejected and persecuted, and that this will be a characteristic of the end times: "Ye shall be hated of all men for my name's sake," says the Lord. "But he that endureth to the end shall be saved" (Mat. 10:22).

Hippolytus envisions a scene in which those who have hidden are found out and forced to publicly choose between Christ and Antichrist:

> Then will he send the cohorts of the demons among mountains and caves and dens of the

---

[236] Irenaeus, *Against Heresies*, V:28.

earth, to track out those who have been concealed from his eyes, and to bring them forward to worship him. And those who yield to him he will seal with his seal; but those who refuse to submit to him he will consume with incomparable pains and bitterest torments and machinations, such as never have been, nor have reached the ear of man, nor have been seen by the eye of mortals. Blessed shall they be who overcome the tyrant then. For they shall be set forth as more illustrious and loftier than the first witnesses; for the former witnesses overcame his minions only, but these overthrow and conquer the accuser himself, the son of perdition. With what eulogies and crowns, therefore, will they not be adorned by our King, Jesus Christ"[237]

Nevertheless, Christians should never forget that Christ is *already* victorious, and so shall they be. St. John Chrysostom insists that, though pursued, the Church will never be overcome by evil: "The generation of the faithful shall remain, cut off by none of the things that have been mentioned."[238]

The Shepherd of Hermas portrayed the impending tribulation as a beast in the road who, because of the shepherd's faith, could not harm him:

[237] Hippolytus, *Appendix to the Works of Hippolytus*, XXIX.
[238] John Chrysostom, *Homilies According to the Gospel of St. Matthew*, LXXVII, 1.

Then the sun shone out a little, and behold, I see a huge beast like some sea-monster, and from its mouth fiery locusts issued forth. And the beast was about a hundred feet in length, and its head was as it were of pottery. And I began to weep, and to entreat the Lord that He would rescue me from it. Now the beast was coming on with such a rush, that it might have ruined a city. I come near it, and, huge monster as it was, it stretcheth itself on the ground, and merely put forth its tongue, and stirred not at all until I had passed by it.[239]

As in the earliest days of apostolic martyrdom, there will be confessors of the faith who boldly defy Antichrist. These will be, in a sense, Christianity's final and ultimate heroes: St. Cyril of Jerusalem writes, "Who then is that blessed man, that shall at that time devoutly witness for Christ? For I say that the martyrs of that time excel all martyrs. For the martyrs hitherto have wrestled with men only; but in the time of Antichrist they shall do battle with Satan in his own person"[240]

These are not necessarily preserved from physical danger, but God guards their spirit, that they may not lose the reward of their Christian witness. "For the Almighty does not absolutely seclude the saints from his temptation," says St. Augustine, "but shelters only their

---

[239] Hermas, *The Shepherd of Hermas*, I, II, III.
[240] Cyril of Jerusalem, *Catechetical Lectures*, XV, 17.

inner man, where faith resides, that by outward temptation they may grow in grace."[241]

Those willing to endure anything for their faith—
even death—are assured a place in the second resurrection: "Ye shall have tribulation ten days: be thou
faithful unto death, and I will give thee a crown of life,"
says the Lord. "He that hath an ear, let him hear what
the Spirit saith unto the churches: He that overcometh
shall not be hurt of the second death" (Rev. 2:10-11).

---

[241] Augustine, *City of God*, XX, 8.

CHAPTER TWELVE
The Eternal Kingdom

The Lord's Second Coming completes the seventh age of human history and initiates the eighth, which is to be the age outside time: "Seven ages of this world are spoken of, that is, from the creation of the heaven and earth till the general consummation and resurrection of men," says John of Damascus.

> For there is a partial consummation, viz., the death of each man: but there is also a general and complete consummation, when the general resurrection of men will come to pass. And the eighth age is the age to come. Everlasting life and everlasting punishment prove that the age or neon to come is unending. For time will not be counted by days and nights even after the resurrection, but there will rather be one day with no evening, wherein the Sun of Justice will shine brightly on the just, but for the sinful there will be night profound and limitless.[242]

This is not the thousand-year reign of Christ on earth, during which time the good and bad were allowed to coexist, but rather timeless communion with the Holy Spirit and heavenly host, including the full-

[242] John of Damascus, *An Exact Exposition of the Orthodox Faith*, II, 1.

ness of the Church. St. Cyril of Jerusalem says, "And shouldest thou ever hear that the kingdom of Christ shall have an end abhor the heresy.[243]

Old Testament prophets foresaw the eternal nature of the Lord's everlasting kingdom: "And in the days of these kings shall the God of heaven set up a kingdom, which shall never be destroyed: and the kingdom shall not be left to other people, but it shall break in pieces and consume all these kingdoms" (Dan. 2:44).

Inherit the Kingdom

Christ will bid those to enter who have been prepared for the kingdom, and for whom the kingdom has been prepared. And whereas before they were members or participants in the kingdom, now they shall be inheritors of it: "Then shall the king say unto them on his right hand, Come, ye blessed of my Father, inherit the kingdom prepared for you from the foundation of the world" (Mat. 25:34).

And for whom is the kingdom prepared? It is prepared for those who served and loved others as Christ Himself. Those who showed compassion and mercy, whose hearts and homes were opened to the needy — those who, with their spirits already abiding in paradise, brought heaven down to earth. Hippolytus says,

---

[243] Cyril of Jerusalem, *Catechetical Lectures*, XV, 27.

Come, ye blessed of my Father, inherit the kingdom prepared for you, ye who esteemed not riches, ye who had compassion on the poor, who aided the orphans, who helped the widows, who gave drink to the thirsty, who fed the hungry, who received strangers, who clothed the naked, who visited the sick, who comforted those in prison, who helped the blind, who kept the seal of the faith inviolate, who assembled yourselves together in the churches, who listened to my Scriptures, who longed for my words, who observed my law day and night, who endured hardness with me like good soldiers, seeking to please me, your heavenly King. Come, inherit the kingdom prepared for you from the foundation of the world. Behold, my kingdom is made ready; behold, paradise is opened; behold, my immortality is shown in its beauty. Come all, inherit the kingdom prepared for you from the foundation of the world.[244]

The Kingdom Filled

Heaven shall be filled with the souls of those who labored for Christ, whether their efforts began early or late, from the first even to the eleventh hour. "And they shall come from the east, and from the west, and from the north, and from the south, and shall sit down in the kingdom of God. And behold, there are last which shall

---

[244] Hippolytus, *Appendix to the Works of Hippolytus*, XLII.

be first, and there are first which shall be last" (Luke 13: 29-30).

In eternity believers will glow with the uncreated light of God. That which before had been hidden by the cloak of the flesh shall be revealed — holiness as light, evil as darkness: "Then the righteous shall shine forth like the sun, while the wicked shall be shown to be mute and gloomy," says Hippolytus. "For both the righteous and the wicked shall be raised incorruptible: the righteous, to be honoured eternally, and to taste immortal joys; and the wicked, to be punished in judgment eternally."[245]

Reward for Long Labors

Finally man will be able to see things as they are. No more shall he be deceived by the passing and unreal appearance of things, but rather he shall perceive truth in all. He will understand himself, and (to the degree that God allows) understand the spiritual nature of creation.

> I am the friend of man, but yet also a righteous Judge to all. For I shall award the recompense according to desert; I shall give the reward to all, according to each man's labour; I shall make return to all, according to each man's conflict. I wish to have pity, but I see no oil in your vessels. I desire to have mercy, but ye have passed through life entirely without mercy. I long to

[245] Hippolytus, *Appendix to the Works of Hippolytus,* XXXIX.

have compassion, but your lamps are dark by reason of your hardness of heart. Depart from me. For judgment is without mercy to him that hath showed no mercy.[246]

Finally man will commune with his brother angels: those who are saved will rejoice in the companionship of the blessed spirits attending God's throne, while those who are damned will writhe in the accursed presence of the fallen angels with whom they conspired during earthly life. "Those men who have been embraced by God's grace, and are become the fellow-citizens of the holy angels who have continued in bliss, shall never more either sin or die, being endued with spiritual bodies," says Augustine. "Yet being clothed with immortality, such as the angels enjoy, of which they cannot be divested...the nature of their flesh shall continue the same, but all carnal corruption and unwieldiness shall be removed."[247]

In eternity, each human soul will be reunited with the body in which it obtained either salvation or damnation, as St. Gregory Palamas wrote,

> The Son of God, who in His compassion became man, died so far as His body was concerned when His soul was separated from His body; but this body was not separated from His divinity, and so He raised up His body once more and took it with Him to heaven in glory. Similarly, when those who have lived

[246] Hippolytus, *Appendix to the Works of Hippolytus*, XLVII.
[247] Augustine, *City of God*, p. 440.

here in a godly manner are separated from their bodies, they are not separated from God, and in the resurrection they will take their bodies with them to God, and in their bodies they will enter with inexpressible joy there where Jesus has preceded us (cf. Heb. 6:20) and in their bodies they will enjoy the glory that will be revealed in Christ (cf. 1 Pet. 5:1). Indeed, they will share not only in resurrection, but also in the Lord's ascension and in all divine life.[248]

Heaven and Earth Shaken

And, like these new spirits, purged of what was foreign to them and brought into the angelic state, a new heaven and a new earth will be formed:

Now he has promised, saying, Yet once more I shake not the earth only, but also heaven. And this word, yet once more, signifieth the removing of those things which are shaken, as of things that are made, that those things which cannot be shaken may remain. Wherefore we receiving a kingdom which cannot be moved, let us have grace, whereby we may serve God acceptably with reverence and godly fear (Heb. 12:26-28).

[248] Gregory Palamas, "To the Most Reverend Nun Xenia" 15, *The Philokalia*, Vol. 4, edited by Palmer, Sherrard and Ware; Faber and Faber, p. 298.

But this shaking of the earth will not disturb the saints. Augustine indicates that the burning and purging will be of no consequence to those have been raised in the Second Resurrection:

> And by this universal conflagration the qualities of the corruptible elements which suited our corruptible bodies shall utterly perish, and our substance shall receive such qualities as shall, by a wonderful transmutation, harmonize with our immortal bodies, so that, as the world itself is renewed to some better thing, it is fitly accommodated to men, themselves renewed in their flesh to some better thing.[249]

No More Weeping

How many tears have been shed for departed loved ones throughout mankind's history? Death, being unnatural, rankles in the soul of man. Nothing could be more humiliating than dying. And Christ, Who is humility incarnate, conquers this thing.

> For as in Adam all die, do in Christ shall all be made alive. But every man in his own order: Christ the first fruits; afterward they that are Christ's at his coming. Then cometh the end, when he shall have delivered up the kingdom to God, even the Father; when he shall have put down all rule and all authority and power. For

[249] Augustine, *City of God*, XX, 16.

he must reign, till he hath put all enemies under his feet. The last enemy that shall be destroyed is death (1 Cor. 15:23-26).

That there should be no more crying, no more sorrow, but instead only joy—how can the mind of man imagine such bliss? Although Christ reigns now, we understand that this state can only belong to that time of eternal peace in God.

Though this book is called the Apocalypse, there are in it many obscure passages to exercise the mind of the reader, and there are few passages so plain as to assist us in the interpretation of the others, even though we take pains; and this difficulty is increased by the repetition of the same things, in forms so different, that the things referred to seem to be different, although in fact they are only differently stated. But in the words, "God shall wipe away all tears from their eyes; and there shall be no more death, neither sorrow, nor crying, but there shall be no more pain," there is so manifest a reference to the future world and the immortality and eternity of the saints—for only then and only there shall such a condition be realized—that if we think this obscure, we need not expect to find anything plain in any part of Scripture.[250]

---

[250] Cf. Augustine, *City of God*, XX, 17.